A GUIDE
TO
HOUSING LAW

Roger Sproston

Emeraldpublishing.co.uk
www.emeraldpublishing.co.uk

Emerald Guides
Brighton BN2 4EG

British Library Cataloguing in Publication data. A Catalogue record of this book is available from the British Library.

ISBN 9781847161567

Printed by GNP Digital Printing Essex

Contents

Introduction

INTRODUCTION

This revised edition of A Guide to Housing Law, written in the context of a severe recession, is a comprehensive overview of housing across all tenures and is aimed specifically at the layperson, although it can be utilised by the professional.

Housing is very complex and affects all people at some point in their lives. Housing law is ever changing and knowledge of it is usually outside the scope of the layperson. Specialist workers and advisers are needed to make sense of the maze. There is the problem of homelessness and what to do at this traumatic time. How do local authorities work and what are their obligations towards the individual? What is the role of housing associations and housing co-operatives and how can one gain access to this type of property?

In addition, what happens if a person is subject to domestic violence and flees home? What are the obligations of local authorities and housing associations at this time? What happens if a relationship breaks down, what are the rights and obligations of the respective parties at a time like this?

A Guide to Housing Law covers all areas in relation to housing. The rights of the private tenant are covered in depth, along with the rights and obligations of the public sector tenant.

Owner occupation is also covered in depth, in particular the rights and obligations of the leaseholder. The roles of intermediaries are covered along with mortgages and other aspects of owning a home.

A Guide to Housing Law is an extremely comprehensive guide to all aspects of housing and should prove invaluable to all.

1

HOUSING RIGHTS GENERALLY

Whether to rent or buy

Although we are now witnessing prices going down, buying a home in most areas is still only an option for those who can afford the prices and get a mortgage. We are in a market where the majority of first time buyers are still excluded from buying a home. There are advantages to buying a property, if you can. They are as follows:

- When buying you will have a wider choice of property and areas, obviously depending on the price range you can afford.
- You will have more control over your home than when renting.
- You can only normally lose your home if you do not keep up your mortgage repayments.
- In the longer term, it can be cheaper than renting and over the years you will build up equity in the property until you eventually own it.

There are disadvantages to owning, as follows:
- The costs in the early years are usually higher than renting a property, particularly from a local authority or housing association, although usually lower than the private sector.
- There is an initial high cost to buying a house, whereas this is not the case with rented property.
- As an owner-occupier you will be responsible for all repairs and maintenance which can be expensive.
- There is very limited help with your housing costs if your income drops.

Obviously, the ideal landlord from whom to rent is a local authority or a housing association. The advantages of this are:

- Costs are usually lower than the private sector and rents are regulated.
- If your income drops you are usually eligible for housing benefit.
- Most of the repairs and maintenance will be carried out by the landlord, from rental income.
- You will only lose your home if you breach the terms of the tenancy agreement.
- The public sector is non-profit making and will usually be good landlords.

There are disadvantages to renting from a local authority or housing association:

- In some areas there is a very long waiting list for properties. When you eventually are housed it may not be in an area of choice.
- The rent will gradually increase, reaching levels higher than those who own and you will not build up any equity in your property.

Private landlords have increased greatly over the last 15 years, particularly with the advent of buy-to-let, although this sector is in trouble now. There are some advantages to renting from a private landlord. They are:

- There will be a wider choice of areas and properties than in the public sector, if you have the means to rent them.
- There is rarely a waiting list.
- You can get help with your rent if your income drops.
- Most of the repairs and maintenance will be met by the landlord out of rent.

There are, as always, disadvantages to renting in the private sector:

- Rents can be very high.
- Rent will go up over time, usually more than the public sector.
- Tenants in the private sector have limited protection. In the public sector, tenancies are usually for life, subject to breach of

contract. Homeowners own the property they live in. Private sector tenants are in the weakest position.

Different types of house and tenancy will suit different people at different times of their lives, depending on their circumstances. There are many things to consider when making a decision, these being outlined below.

Renting from a local authority

Council homes are, along with housing association property and, in some cases, housing co-operatives, the most affordable type of housing. The allocation of council housing will depend on your need and those in the most need will usually be given priority over others. This has been a bone of contention for many years, however, need is measured in a scientific way, with points allocated according to different circumstances.

You can find out from the council housing department about how to go about making an application for housing. If you are being actively considered for an offer of housing then the council will usually send someone to visit you. In most cases, it is necessary to reregister on the housing register each year, in order to keep an active list of those in need.

The housing register

Councils will keep a list, or register of people who apply for housing. This has been a requirement for some years now. This register is also sometimes known as a 'waiting list' although this is misleading since length of time on the list is certainly not the only factor taken into account when it comes to being rehoused.

There are four main ways in which councils will decide who goes to the top of the list:

- Point's scheme. These are commonly used by councils, the aim of the point's scheme being to assess the level of need of the applicants by allocating points based on different factors such as medical needs, number of children, size of present accommodation etc.
- Group schemes. These schemes put applicants into different groups and then allocate a number of homes to each group. The

groups typically might be based on type of household, such as single people, elderly etc, or might be based on conditions such as overcrowding

- Date order schemes. At its simplest this is first come first served.
- Merit schemes. These schemes are rare and each case is assessed on its 'merit'.

Some local authorities will use a combination of these schemes when deciding on allocating housing. An increasingly larger number of local authorities are experimenting with schemes to give more choice by advertising vacancies for which applicants can put in a bid for properties displayed and those in the greatest need or who have been waiting longest will get the property.

A council can decide that a person is not eligible for housing if they have been guilty of behaviour that would entitle them to evict that person as a council tenant.

People arriving from abroad

Some people from abroad are not allowed to register on the housing list. This includes people who are subject to immigration control, people who are allowed to stay subject to not benefiting from public funds and sponsored immigrants who have been in the United Kingdom for less than five years. Also, people who fail the habitual residence test for welfare benefits or who are in breach of EU Rights of Residence Directive. If a local authority refuses to put your name on the housing register, you have the right to ask them to review their decision within 21 days. There are special arrangements for asylum seekers who will be directed towards accommodation in limited areas of the country.

Homeless people

Local authorities have a legal duty to help those who are homeless or threatened with homelessness.

Who is homeless or threatened with homelessness?

People are homeless if:

- They have no accommodation available for them to occupy, including any accommodation in another country, or
- They have a home but are in danger of violence or from threats of violence or

- They are a family who are normally together, but are now living in separate homes because they have nowhere to live together or
- Their accommodation is moveable (e.g. caravan, houseboat) and they have nowhere to place it or
- They have accommodation but it is not reasonable to continue to occupy it.

Not all people who are homeless or threatened with homelessness are provided with a home by the council. The council is, however, under a legal obligation to make sure that homeless people have somewhere to live if:

- They are eligible for assistance (this excludes people from abroad)
- They are in priority need and
- They did not make themselves intentionally homeless.

Priority need

The following groups are counted as being in priority need:

- People who have dependant children aged 16 or under or under 19 if they are receiving full time education or training.
- All pregnant women
- People who are homeless because of a fire or flood or similar emergency.
- People who are vulnerable as a result of old age, mental illness or handicap, physical disability or other special reasons.
- People who are vulnerable as a result of having served in the armed forces, having been in custody, becoming homeless as a result of violence or threats of violence which are likely to be carried out.

The following groups are also seen as vulnerable:

- 16 and 17 year old people, unless they have left care, in which case social services are already responsible for their well-being.
- 18-21 year old young people who have been looked after by social services in the past.

Local councils will always decide who is vulnerable but should always accept people over retirement age. Some will also accept people approaching retirement age if they are in poor health. Councils must act reasonably when making a decision.

Intentionally homeless

If the local authority decides that you are intentionally homeless then this means that they are satisfied that you have given up accommodation you could have continued to live in, or that you have lost accommodation through your own fault, such as non-payment of rent. However, if you are in priority need the council must find you somewhere to live temporarily whilst it makes its decision. It must also give you help and advice with finding your own accommodation.

If you have a home but are about to lose it, it is very important that you stay there as long as you can. If you leave earlier then the council will probably find that you are intentionally homeless.

If you are not in priority need

If you are homeless but not in priority need, then the council does not have a legal obligation to help you. It does however, have the duty to provide advice and assistance.

If you are homeless, or likely to become homeless in the near future, you should go to the Homeless Persons section of the council. This will usually be in the housing department. If you cannot find it then you should go to the nearest council office or the town hall. When you get there, make sure that you are seen by someone from the Homeless Persons section. Tell that person that you are either homeless or are about to become homeless. Make it very clear that you need urgent help and are not there to put your name on the housing register.

Which council to go to

Usually you should go to the council in the area where you became homeless or are about to become homeless. However, long term help for people in priority need is usually offered by the council with whom you have a 'local connection.' Generally, you should be considered as having a local connection if you, or anyone living with you:

- Have lived in the councils area for six months out of the past year, or three years out of the past five, or

12

- Have work (including voluntary work) or
- Have close family who have lived in the area for at least five years or
- Have any other special connection with the area, for example were brought up there.

Residence with or employment with the armed forces doers not count as local connection, nor does residence in a prison, hospital or other institution if you have been staying in one of these. If you apply to a council with which you (or anybody who lives with you) have any of these local connections then that council should be responsible for helping you.

If you have no local connection with the council to which you apply, then that council must investigate your application and decide whether you are homeless, and in priority need, and whether you are intentionally homeless. If it decides that you have a right to help, but have no local connection with the council then it can contact another council with which you have a local connection to make sure it will help you. If you have a local connection with more than one other council and you would prefer to live in a particular area then your wishes should be taken into account. If you have no local connection with any area, then the council to which you apply has the duty to help you. People in fear of domestic violence must never be sent back to the area from which they fled unless the council is satisfied that there is no risk of violence if they return.

The council's investigations

When you ask a council for help because you are homeless they will check:

- Whether you are homeless
- Whether you are eligible for assistance
- Whether you are in priority need
- Whether you are intentionally homeless
- Whether you have a local connection with the area

These investigations often involve detailed questions about your own personal life.

People who withhold personal information or give wrong information can be prosecuted and fined.

If you have nowhere to live whilst the council is checking out your story it must make sure that you are adequately temporarily housed. If the council finds that it has no duty to house you then it should provide reasons in writing.

Councils may put homeless people initially into emergency or temporary accommodation. This can be a room in a bed and breakfast hotel, a hostel, a house waiting to be demolished or improved or a home rented from a private landlord. If you have furniture and cannot take it or store it then the council must provide a safe place for it. They can make a reasonable charge.

Eventually, the council should offer you a permanent home. This may or may not be a council house or flat and may be their least desirable stock. You should be careful about turning down an offer of accommodation as the council can state that they have discharged their duty. You can ask them to review their decision. You should normally ask for a review within 21 days of being told about the decision. If the council does not change its decision then it must give reasons. If you disagree with the council's decision you might be able to challenge it if you believe that the council has misinterpreted the law, has reached a grossly unreasonable decision or has not taken proper account of the facts.

Extra help for homeless young people

Young people aged less than 18 years have extra rights from social services in addition to rights under homeless person's legislation. They have a duty to provide accommodation to any young person who is homeless and in need and whose welfare is otherwise likely to be seriously prejudiced. A young person is counted as being in need if they are unlikely to be able to achieve or maintain a reasonable standard of health or development without the provision of services by the council, or if their health or development is likely to be impaired, or if they have a disability. Social services will often meet this obligation by asking the local authority to help. Social services also have a duty towards young persons coming out of care. They have a duty to provide accommodation and support for all 16 and 17 year olds coming out of care. Social services also have power (but not a duty) to provide accommodation for young people aged under 21 if that would promote or safeguard their welfare.

Other rights to re-housing

People who lose their homes as a result of action by the local authority will, usually, have a right to re-housing. Councils may make a compulsory purchase order on a house and then demolish it, councils may decide that a property needs improving and occupiers have to move out permanently. If this is the case then there is a right to re-housing. Anyone legally living in the property at the time of these actions is entitled to re-housing, the right applying to owners or tenants. It does not apply to those moving in after the action has commenced or to squatters.

People who have to vacate their homes in these circumstances can also claim home loss payment to a maximum of £15,000, (check current figures with your local authority as they are subject to change) disturbance payment to help with the costs of moving and a well-maintained payment which involves a payment to the owners or tenants if the property is to be compulsory purchased and has been well maintained up to the time of compulsory purchase.

Other council housing schemes in operation

In addition to those schemes outlined above, councils have a number of other schemes in operation. The most common area:

Hard-to-let or low-demand schemes. This is where the council has unpopular homes in areas that are blighted for example, or in tower blocks. Property like this is typically offered to low priority groups such as young single people.

Schemes for special groups-Some council's have quotas for special groups, such as for those with special needs, mental illness etc.

Transferring to another council house

If you want to move within a local authority area you can apply for a transfer. There are usually more people wanting transfers for a variety of different reasons than there is property available. Councils will prioritise transfers and usually allocate points to people depending on circumstances. These circumstances vary and can be for overcrowding to racial harassment and domestic violence. A transfer will be decided upon after looking at circumstances. If a person has had to flee due to domestic violence, or has an urgent medical need then they will be afforded higher priority than a family who need more bedrooms. Usually, with the exception of those in emergency need there is a long wait for a transfer. Transfers can also be effected outside of local authority areas through liaison with other councils and local authorities.

Exchanging properties

Tenants of public sector housing, at least secure and assured tenants, have the right to exchange their homes with another person or family, subject to permission from the landlord, which cannot be unreasonably withheld. There are a number of reasons why the council or association can refuse to let an exchange go ahead:

- There is a court order to evict one of the applicants
- There is impending possession proceedings
- The accommodation you want to transfer is larger than your needs (substantially larger)
- The accommodation is too small
- The landlord is a charity and the proposed new tenant does not suit the aims and objectives of the landlord
- Accommodation is specially adapted for a person with physical disabilities and the proposed new tenant is not disabled.
- The accommodation is managed by a tenant management co-operative and the proposed tenant does not want to become part of the co-operative.

There are a number of ways of finding a tenant to exchange with you:
- Various Tenants Exchange Schemes, details of which can be obtained from the internet. You can also obtain details from your landlord.
- Councils usually keep lists of those who want to exchange
- Advertise in the local papers and shop windows in the area you want to move to.

Housing associations

Housing associations and housing trusts are slightly different to councils in their make up. Although publicly funded and accountable to a board of management and to the Tenant Services Authority, which is a quango set up by Parliament to regulate the activities of associations, they are more independent than councils.

Housing associations will offer a variety of tenancy types, some not offered by councils. However, they will work closely with the local authority when it comes to receiving nominations and referrals for housing. Often, they are only permitted to develop in a local authority area if they agree an ongoing quota of nominations from councils. Many associations will only house those on the housing register. However, if you have a problem getting onto the housing register then you should seek advice form the council.

Housing associations which are registered with the TSA are obliged by law to give details of how they allocate tenancies. Some associations will take direct applications others will work through agencies. It depends on the associations.

Housing association tenancies are usually assured and assured shorthold, with some secure, usually created out of an exchange. However, as we will see a little later, housing associations have not been able to grant secure tenancies since January 1st 1989 and therefore, the secure tenancy, which is now a local authority tenancy only, is dwindling in associations.

Renting from a private landlord

If you cannot afford to buy a property, as a lot of people cannot due to rising house prices, and you do not qualify for a council or housing association tenancy then you will need to do as a growing number of people do, and that is rent from a private landlord. This is usually the most expensive way of renting but there is usually availability of property.

The majority of private lets are found through local estate agents with a letting arm. They will advertise property and vet prospective tenants, taking up references and also provide a management service to the landlord that can cost anything between 10-15% of rental income plus VAT. Many agencies will charge the tenant a fee for drawing up a tenancy but are not allowed to charge a deposit before a property is found. On finding a property you will need to pay a deposit which is returnable. The deposit is now protected by the Tenancy Deposit Protection Scheme, introduced in 2007. Renting a property is outlined in more depth further on in the book.

Housing co-operatives

Housing co-operatives consist of groups of people who each have a share in the overall co-op, usually a £1 share and each have a responsibility for managing the co-op, usually delegated to a committee. Individuals are expected to show an active interest and participate in the day-to-day running. Co-ops will allocate their own property but will also sometimes have agreements with local authorities. Three are relatively few co-ops in existence and they are difficult to get into.

2

THE LAW AND MOBILE HOMES

If you own a mobile home, rent a pitch for it on a site and use it as your main residence, you will be protected by the Mobile Homes Act 1983. If you rent the home you will be covered by the law for tenants. The Act does not cover you if you only rent the home for holidays.

Protection from eviction
The Mobile Homes Act 1983 gives owners the right to keep their homes on the site they occupy indefinitely. There can only be a fixed time limit on the agreement if the site owner's planning permission, or right to use the land, is itself limited to a fixed period. If the time limit is later extended, then so is your right to stay there. The resident can bring the agreement to an end by giving at least four weeks notice in writing. The site owner can only bring the agreement to an end by applying to the county court or to an arbitrator. There are only three grounds on which the site owner can seek to end an agreement:

- You are not living in the mobile home as your main residence.
- The mobile home is having a detrimental effect on the site because of its age or condition or is likely to have this effect within the next five years. The site owner can only try to use this ground for ending the agreement once in any five-year period, starting from the date the agreement began.
- You have broken one of the terms of the agreement and the court or the arbitrator thinks it is reasonable to end the agreement. The site owner must first tell you that you have broken the agreement and give you a reasonable time to put things right.

If the site owner can prove to the court or the arbitrator that the agreement should be brought to an end for one of these reasons, the site owner can then get an eviction order from the courts. Arbitrators cannot make eviction orders. The site owner can normally go to court to end the agreement and for an eviction order at the same time.

If the site is privately owned, the court can suspend an eviction order for up to one year, but cannot suspend it if the site is owned by the local council. It is a criminal offence for the site owner to evict you without a court order, to harass or threaten you or to cut off services such as gas, electricity or water in order to get you to leave.

The site owner can only make you move to another part of the site if:

- Your agreement says that this can be done
- The new pitch is broadly comparable to the old one
- The site owner pays all the costs.

The right to a written agreement and a statement of rights

The site owner must give you a statement of your legal rights and the terms of your agreement. The agreement cannot change your rights under the Mobile Homes Act. You or the site owner can apply to change the terms of the agreement within six months of the issue of the original agreement. Either side can apply to the county court or an arbitrator, if they cannot agree the terms. You should always check the agreement for the terms of payment and fees and, if you are not happy, apply to change them.

Other rights of mobile home owners

You can sell your home and pass on the agreement with the site owner to a person of your choice. You can also give your home to a member of your family. In either case, the new owner must be approved by the site owner, but this approval cannot be unreasonably withheld. If this is the case then you can apply to the county court or an arbitrator for an order for the site owner to give approval. If you sell your home the site owner can claim a commission of up to 20% of the price. If you die members of your family who were living with you will automatically inherit the agreement with the site owner and your legal rights.

3

PRIVATE TENANTS
FINDING A PROPERTY

Letting Agents

When looking for a property, there are obvious advantages in using an agent: they are likely to be experienced, can provide you with a tenancy agreement and they can provide a service after the property is let. It is important for a tenant to know that there will be a proper relationship between him/her and the landlord after moving in. Managing agents will provide this link.

Agents will typically look after the following:

- Transfer the utility bills and the council tax into the name of the tenant.
- Pay for repairs, although an agent will only normally do this if rent is being paid directly to them and they can make appropriate deductions.
- Chase rent arrears
- Serve notices of intent to seek possession if the landlord instructs them to do. An agent cannot commence court proceedings except through a solicitor.
- Visit the property at regular intervals check that the tenants are not causing any damage.
- Deal with neighbour complaints
- Bank rental receipts if the landlord is abroad
- Deal with housing benefit departments if necessary.

The extent to which agents actually do any or all of the following really depends on the calibre of the agent. It also depends on the type of agreement the landlord has with the agent.

Beware! There are many rental agencies. These agents are not all professional, many do not know a thing about property management and are shady and should be avoided like the plague. Shop around and seek a reputable agent.

Advertisements

The classified advertisement section of local papers is a good place to seek a property. Local papers are obviously cheaper than the nationals such as the Evening Standard in London or the broadsheets such as the Guardian. The type of newspaper you look in will largely reflect what type of property you are looking for. An advert in the pages of the Times would indicate that the landlord is looking for a well-heeled professional and this would be reflected in the type of property that is to let.

Company lets

Where the tenant is a company rather than an individual, the tenancy agreement will be similar to an assured shorthold, but will not be bound by the six-month rule (see chapter 7 for details of assured shorthold tenancies). Company lets can be from any length of time, from a week to several years, or as long as you like.

The major difference between contracts and standard assured shorthold agreements is that the contract will be tailored to individual needs, and the agreement is bound by the provisions of contract law. Company tenancies are bound by the provisions of contract law and not by the 1988 Housing Act. Note: if you are a company and you are looking for a property to rent let you must use a letting agent or solicitor. Most landlords will insist on it.

The advantages of a landlord letting to a company are:

- A company or embassy has no security of tenure and therefore cannot be a sitting tenant.
- A company cannot seek to reduce the rent by statutory interventions.
- Rental payments are often made quarterly or six monthly in advance.
- The financial status of a company is usually more secure than that of an individual.

- Company tenants often require long-term lets to accommodate staff relocating on contracts of between one and five years.

The main disadvantages of company lets are:

- A company tenancy can only be to a bona fide company or embassy, not to a private individual.
- A tenancy to a partnership would not count as a company let and may have some security of tenure.
- If the tenant is a foreign government, the diplomatic status of the occupant must be ascertained, as the courts cannot enforce breaches of contract with somebody who possesses diplomatic immunity.
- A tenancy to a foreign company not registered in the U.K may prove time consuming and costly if it becomes necessary to pursue claims for unpaid rent or damage through foreign courts.

Short-lets

Although company lets can be of any length, it is becoming increasingly popular for companies to rent flats from private landlords on short-lets.

A short let is any let of less than six months. But here, it is essential to check the rules with the local authority concerned. Some boroughs will not allow lets for less than three months, as they do not want to encourage transient people in the neighbourhood.

Generally speaking, short-lets are only applicable in large cities where there is a substantial shifting population. Business executives on temporary relocation, actors and others involved in television production or film work, contract workers and visiting academics are examples of people who might require a short-let.

From a landlord's point of view, short-lets are an excellent idea if you have to vacate your own home for seven or eight months, say, and do not want to leave it empty for that time. Short-let tenants provide useful extra income as well as keeping an eye on the place. Or, if you are buying a new property and have not yet sold the old one, it can make good business sense to let it to a short-let tenant.

Short-let tenants are, usually, from a landlord's point of view, excellent blue-chip occupants. They are busy professionals, high earners, out all day and used to high standards. As the rent is paid by the company there is no worry for the landlord on this score either.

A major plus of short-lets is that they command between 20-50% more rent than the optimum market rent for that type of property. The one downside of short-lets is that no agency can guarantee permanent occupancy.

Student lets

Many letting agencies will not consider students and a lot of landlords similarly are not keen. There is the perception that students will not look after a home and tend to live a lifestyle guaranteed to increase the wear and tear on a property. However, if handled correctly, student lets can be profitable. Although students quite often want property for only eight or nine months, agencies that deal with students make them sign for a whole year. Rent is guaranteed by confirmation that the student is a genuine student with references from parents, who act as guarantors.

There can be a lot of money made from student lets. However, the tenancy will require more avid policing because of the nature of student lifestyle.

The DSS and housing benefit

Very few letting agencies or landlords will touch DSS or housing benefits tenants. However, as with student lets, there is another side of the coin.

Quite often it is essential for a tenant on HB to have a guarantor, usually a homeowner, before signing a tenancy. Then it is up to the machinations of the benefit system to ensure that the landlord receives rent. The rent is assessed by a benefit officer, with the rent estimated usually at market price. There are rent levels set for each are that the benefit officer will not go above.

A deposit is paid normally and rent is paid direct to the landlord. No other conditions can be accepted by a private landlord. Rent certainly cannot be paid direct to the tenant.

Although tenants on HB have a bad name, due to stereotyping, there are many reasons why a person may be on benefit and probably does not fit the picture of a scrounger who will trash a property. If housing benefit tenancies are managed well, then this can be a useful source of tenant.

Holiday-lets

Before the Housing Act 1988 became law, many landlords advertised their properties as holiday-lets to bypass the rules regarding security of tenure. Strictly speaking, a holiday-let is a property let for no more than a month to any one tenant. If the same tenant renews for another month then the landlord is breaking the law. Nowadays, holiday-lets must be just that-let for a genuine holiday.

Holiday-lets are not covered by the Housing Act. The contract is finalized by exchange of letters with the tenant where they place a deposit and the owner confirms the booking. If the let is not for a genuine holiday you may have problems in evicting the tenant, as the whole point of a holiday let is that it is for no more than a fixed period of a month.

Generally speaking, certain services must be provided for the let to be deemed a holiday-let. Cleaning services and changes of bed linen are essential. The amount paid by the holidaymaker will usually include utilities but would exclude use of the telephone, fax machine etc.

If possible, you should talk to someone with some experience of this type of let before entering into an agreement with an agency. The usual problems may arise, those of ensuring occupancy all year round and the maintenance of your property, which will be higher due to a high turnover.

Bed-sits

Bed-sitting rooms are usually difficult to let and can cause problems for tenants as well as landlords. It is best to leave this area of letting alone. There are numerous regulations to adhere to, Houses in Multiple Occupation regulations are quite strict. There is a problem also of high turnover. Leave this kind of letting to others and concentrate on houses or flats.

Viewing a property

Once you have found a property, the next stage is to make arrangements for a viewing. It is a good idea to make all appointments on the same day in order to avoid wasting time. If you decide on a likely property, the landlord will wish to take up references, if an agency is not being used. This will normally be a previous landlord's reference and also a bank reference. Only when these have been received and it is established that the person(s) are safe will the letting go ahead. No keys will be handed over until the cheque has been cleared and the landlord is in receipt of a month's rent and a month's deposit.

Deposits

Tenancy deposit protection scheme

The Tenancy Deposit Protection Scheme was introduced to protect all deposits paid to landlords after 6th April 2007. After this date, landlords and/or agents must use a government authorised scheme to protect deposits. The need for such a scheme has arisen because of the historical problem with deposits and the abuse of deposits by landlords.

The scheme works as follows:

Moving into a property

At the beginning of a new tenancy agreement, the tenant will pay a deposit to the landlord or agent as usual. Within 14 days the landlord is required to give the tenant details of how the deposit is going to be protected including:

- the contact details of the tenancy deposit scheme
- the contact details of landlord or agent
- how to apply for the release of the deposit
- what to do if there is a dispute about the deposit

There are three tenancy deposit schemes that your landlord can opt for:

Tenancy Deposit Solutions Ltd
info@mydeposits.co.uk

The Tenancy Deposit Scheme
www.tds.gb.com
0845 226 7837
The Deposit Protection Service
www.depositprotection.com
0870 707 1 707

The schemes above fall into two categories, insurance based schemes and custodial schemes.

Custodial Scheme

- The tenant pays the deposit to the landlord
- The landlord pays the deposit into the scheme
- Within 14 days of receiving the deposit, the landlord must give the tenant prescribed information
- A the end of the tenancy, if the landlord and tenant have agreed how much of the deposit is to be returned, they will tell the scheme which returns the deposit, divided in the way agreed by the parties.
- If there is a dispute, the scheme will hold the disputed amount until the dispute resolution service or courts decide what is fair
- The interest accrued by deposits in the scheme will be used to pay for the running of the scheme and any surplus will be used to offer interest to the tenant, or landlord if the tenant isn't entitled to it.

Insurance based schemes

- The tenant pays the deposit to the landlord
- The landlord retains the deposit and pays a premium to the insurer (this is the key difference between the two schemes)
- Within 14 days of receiving a deposit the landlord must give the tenant prescribed information.
- At the end of the tenancy if the landlord and tenant agree how the deposit is to be divided or otherwise then the landlord will return the amount agreed
- If there is a dispute, the landlord must hand over the disputed amount to the scheme for safekeeping until the dispute is resolved
- If for any reason the landlord fails to comply, the insurance arrangements will ensure the return of the deposit to the tenant if they are entitled to it.

If your landlord or agent hasn't protected your deposit with one of the above then you can apply to your local county court for an order for the landlord either to protect the deposit or repay it.

Moving out

At the end of the tenancy, check whether you are leaving the property in good order. Allow for fair wear and tear if the condition has deteriorated because of your use. Agree with your landlord how much of the deposit should be returned and within ten days the balance of the deposit or the entire deposit if appropriate will be returned to you.

Resolving disputes

When you move out, if there is a dispute then there will be a free service offered by the elected scheme to help resolve the dispute. It is important to remember that until the dispute is resolved then the deposit will be held by the scheme. It is also important to understand that the landlord cannot give you notice to end the tenancy until he or she has protected the deposit and given you notice as to how it is going to be protected.

For information generally about Tenancy Deposit protection you should visit www.tenancydeposit.gov.uk.

This site will tell you in detail how the whole scheme works.

4

PRIVATE TENANTS AND THE LAW

Explaining the law

As a tenant, or potential tenant, it is very important to understand the rights and obligations of both yourself and your landlord, exactly what can and what cannot be done once the tenancy agreement has been signed and you have moved into the property.

Some landlords think they can do exactly as they please, because the property belongs to them. Some tenants do not know any differently and therefore the landlord can, and often does, get away with breaking the law. However, this is not the case, there is a very strong legal framework governing the relationship between landlord and tenant and it is important that you have a grasp on the key principles of the law.

In order to fully understand the law we should begin by looking at the main types of relationship between people and their homes.

The freehold and the lease

In law, there are two main types of ownership and occupation of property. These are: freehold and leasehold. These arrangements are very old indeed.

Freehold

If a person owns their property outright (usually with a mortgage) then they are a freeholder. The only claims to ownership over and above their own might be those of the building society or the bank, which lent them the money to buy the place. They will re-possess the property if the mortgage payments are not kept up with.

In certain situations though, the local authority (council) for an area can affect a person's right to do what they please with their home even if they are a freeholder. This will occur when planning powers are exercised, for example, in order to prevent the carrying out of alterations without consent.

The local authority for your area has many powers and we will be referring to these regularly.

Leasehold

If a person lives in a property owned by someone else and has a written agreement allowing them to occupy the flat or house for a period of time i.e., giving them permission to live in that property, then they will, in the main, have a lease and either be a leaseholder or a tenant of a landlord.

The main principle of a lease is that a person has been given permission by someone else to live in his or her property for a period of time. The person giving permission could be either the freeholder or another leaseholder.

The tenancy agreement is one type of lease. If you have signed a tenancy agreement then you will have been given permission by a person to live in their property for a period of time.

The position of the tenant

The tenant will usually have an agreement for a shorter period of time than the typical leaseholder. Whereas the leaseholder will, for example, have an agreement for ninety-nine years, the tenant will have an agreement, which either runs from week to week or month to month (periodic tenancy) or is for a fixed term, for example, six-months or one-year.

These arrangements are the most common types of agreement between the private landlord and tenant.

The agreement itself will state whether it is a fixed-term or periodic tenancy. If an agreement has not been issued it will be assumed to be a fixed term tenancy.

Both periodic and fixed-term tenants will usually pay a sum of rent regularly to a landlord in return for permission to live in the property (more about rent and service charges later)

The tenancy agreement

The tenancy agreement is the usual arrangement under which one person will live in a property owned by another. Before a tenant moves into a property he/she will have to sign a tenancy agreement drawn up by a landlord or landlord's agent. *A tenancy agreement is a contract between landlord and tenant.*

It is important to realize that when you sign a tenancy agreement, you have signed a contract with another person, which governs the way in which you will live in their property.

The contract

Typically, any tenancy agreement will show the name and address of the landlord and will state the names of the tenant(s). The type of tenancy agreement that is signed should be clearly indicated. This could be, for example, a Rent Act protected tenancy, an assured tenancy or an assured shorthold tenancy. In the main, in the private sector, the agreement will be an assured shorthold.

Date of commencement of tenancy and rent payable

The date the tenancy began and the duration (fixed term or periodic) plus the amount of rent payable should be clearly shown, along with who is responsible for any other charges, such as water rates, council tax etc, and a description of the property you are living in. The landlord must also serve a notice stating the address to where any legal notices can be sent.

In addition to the rent that must be paid there should be a clear indication of when a rent increase can be expected. This information is sometimes shown in other conditions of tenancy, which should be given to the tenant when they move into their home.

The conditions of tenancy will set out landlords and tenants rights and obligations.

Services provided under the tenancy and service of notice

If services are provided, i.e., if a service charge is payable, this should be indicated in the agreement. The tenancy agreement, as stated, should indicate clearly the address to which notices on the landlord can be served by the tenant, for example, because of repair problems or notice of leaving the property. The landlord has a legal requirement to indicate this.

Tenants obligations

The tenancy agreement will either be a basic document with the above information or will be more comprehensive. Either way, there will be a section beginning "the tenant agrees." Here the tenant will agree to move into the property, pay rent, use the property as an only home, not cause a nuisance to others, take responsibility for certain internal repairs, not sublet the property, i.e., create another tenancy, and various other things depending on the property.

Landlords obligations

There should also be another section "the landlord agrees". Here, the landlord is contracting with the tenant to allow quiet enjoyment of the property. The landlord's repairing responsibilities are also usually outlined.

Ending a tenancy

Finally, there should be a section entitled "ending the tenancy" which will outline the ways in which landlord and tenant can end the agreement. It is in this section that the landlord should make reference to the "grounds for possession". Grounds for possession are circumstances where the landlord will apply to court for possession of his/her property. Some of these grounds relate to what is in the tenancy, i.e., the responsibility to pay rent and to not cause a nuisance.

Other grounds do not relate to the contents of the tenancy directly, but more to the law governing that particular tenancy. The grounds for possession are very important, as they are used in any court case brought against the tenant. Unfortunately, they are not always indicated in the tenancy agreement. As they are so important they are summarized later on in this chapter.

It must be said at this point that many residential tenancies are very light on landlord's responsibilities. Repairing responsibilities, and responsibilities relating to rental payment, are landlord's obligations under law. This book deals with these, and other areas. However, many landlords will seek to use only the most basic document in order to conceal legal obligations.

The public sector tenancy (local authority or housing association), for example, is usually very clear and very comprehensive about the rights and obligations of landlord and tenant. Unfortunately, the private landlord often does not employ the same energy when it comes to educating and informing the tenant.

The responsibility of the landlord to provide a tenant with a rent book

If the tenant is a weekly periodic tenant the landlord must provide him/her with a rent book and commits a criminal offence if he/she does not do so. This is outlined in the Landlord and Tenant Act 1985 sections 4 - 7. Under this Act any tenant can ask in writing the name and address of the landlord.

The landlord must reply within twenty-one days of asking.

As most tenancies nowadays are fixed term assured shortholds then it is not strictly necessary to provide a tenant with a rent book. However, for the purposes of efficiency, and your own records, it is always useful to have a rent book and sign it each time rent is collected or a standing order is paid.

Overcrowding and the rules governing too many people living in the property

It is important to understand, when signing a tenancy agreement, that it is not permitted to allow the premises to become overcrowded, i.e., to allow more people than was originally intended, (which is outlined in the agreement) to live in the property. If a tenant does, then the landlord can take action to evict.

Different types of tenancy agreement

The protected tenancy - the meaning of the term

As a basic guide, if a person is a private tenant and signed their current agreement with a landlord before 15th January 1989 then they will, in most cases, be a protected tenant with all the rights relating to protection of tenure, which are considerable. Protection is provided under the 1977 Rent Act.

In practice, there are not many protected tenancies left and the tenant will usually be signing an assured shorthold tenancy..

The assured shorthold tenancy - what it means

If the tenant entered into an agreement with a landlord after 15th January 1989 then they will, in most cases, be an assured tenant. We will discuss assured tenancies in more depth in the next chapter In brief, there are various types of assured tenancy. The assured shorthold is usually a fixed term version of the assured tenancy and enables the landlord to recover their property after six months and to vary the rent after this time.

At this point it is important to understand that the main difference between the two types of tenancy, protected and assured, is that the tenant has less rights as a tenant under the assured tenancy. For example, they will not be entitled, as is a protected tenant, to a fair rent set by a Rent Officer.

Other types of agreement

In addition to the above tenancy agreements, there are other types of agreement sometimes used in privately rented property. One of these is the company let, as we discussed in the last chapter, and another is the license agreement. The person signing such an agreement is called a licensee.

Licenses will only apply in special circumstances where the licensee cannot be given sole occupation of his home and therefore can only stay for a short period with minimum rights.

The squatter (trespasser)

In addition to the tenant and licensee, there is one other type of occupation of property, which needs mentioning. This is squatting. It is useful for the tenant to have a basic understanding of this area of occupation.

The squatter is usually someone who has gained entry to a vacant property, either a house or a flat, without permission.

Although the squatter, a trespasser, has the protection of the law and cannot be evicted without a court order, if he or she is to be given the protection of the law, the squatted property must have been empty in the first place.

On gaining entry to a property, the squatter will normally put up a notice claiming squatter's rights, which means that they are identifying themselves as a person or group having legal protection until a court order is obtained to evict them. Even if no notice is visible, the squatter has protection and it is an offence to attempt to remove them forcibly.

The squatter has protection from eviction under the Protection from Eviction Act 1977 and is also protected from violence or harassment by the Criminal Law Act of 1977.

The trespasser who has entered an occupied property without permission has fewer rights. Usually, the police will either arrest or escort a trespasser off the premises. There is no protection from eviction. However, there is protection from violence and intimidation under the Criminal Law Act of 1977.

5

ASSURED TENANTS

The assured tenant

As we have seen, with the exception of local authority tenancies, all tenancies, (with the main exceptions detailed), are known as assured tenancies. An assured shorthold, which is the most common form of tenancy used by the landlord nowadays, is one type of assured tenancy, and is for a fixed term of six months minimum and can be brought to an end with two months notice by serving a section 21 (of the Housing Act 1988) notice.

It is important to note that all tenancies signed after February 1997 are assured shorthold agreements unless otherwise stated.

Assured tenancies are governed by the 1988 Housing Act, as amended by the 1996 Housing Act. It is to these Acts, or outlines of the Acts that the tenant must refer when intending to sign a tenancy for a residential property.

For a tenancy to be assured, three conditions must be fulfilled:

1. The premises must be a dwelling house. This basically means any premises which can be lived in. Business premises will normally fall outside this interpretation.
2. There must exist a particular relationship between landlord and tenant. In other words there must exist a tenancy agreement. For example, a license to occupy, as in the case of students, or accommodation occupied as a result of work, cannot be seen as a tenancy. Following on from this, the accommodation must be let as a single unit. The tenant, who must be an individual, must normally be able to sleep, cook and eat in the accommodation. Sharing of bathroom facilities will not prevent a tenancy being an assured tenancy but shared cooking or other facilities, such as a living room, will.
3. The third requirement for an assured tenancy is that the tenant must occupy the dwelling as his or her only or principal home. In situations involving joint tenants at least one of them must occupy.

Tenancies that are not assured

A tenancy agreement will not be assured if one of the following conditions applies:

-The tenancy or the contract was entered into before 15th January 1989;

-If no rent is payable or if only a low rent amounting to less than two thirds of the present ratable value of the property is payable;

-If the premises are let for business purposes or for mixed residential and business purposes;

-If part of the dwelling house is licensed for the sale of liquor for consumption on the premises. This does not include the publican who lets out a flat;

-If the dwelling house is let with more than two acres of agricultural land;

-If the dwelling house is part of an agricultural holding and is occupied in relation to carrying out work on the holding;

-If the premises are let by a specified institution to students, i.e., halls of residence;

-If the premises are let for the purpose of a holiday;

-Where there is a resident landlord, e.g., in the case where the landlord has let one of his rooms but continues to live in the house;

-If the landlord is the Crown (the monarchy) or a government department. Certain lettings by the Crown are capable of being assured, such as some lettings by the Crown Estate Commissioners;

-If the landlord is a local authority, a fully mutual housing association (this is where you have to be a shareholder to be a tenant) a newly created Housing Action Trust or any similar body listed in the 1988 Housing Act.

-If the letting is transitional such as a tenancy continuing in its original form until phased out, such as:

-A protected tenancy under the 1977 Rent Act;

-Secure tenancy granted before 1st January 1989, e.g., from a local authority or housing association. These tenancies are governed by the 1985 Housing Act).

The Assured Shorthold tenancy

The assured shorthold tenancy as we have seen, is the most common form of tenancy used in the private sector. The main principle of the assured shorthold tenancy is that it is issued for a period of six months minimum and can be brought to an end by the landlord serving two-months notice on the tenant. At the end of the six-month period the tenant, if given two months prior notice, must leave.

Any property let on an assured tenancy can be let on an assured shorthold, providing the following three conditions are met:

- The tenancy must be for a fixed term of not less than six months.
- The agreement cannot contain powers which enable the landlord to end the tenancy before six months. This does not include the right of the landlord to enforce the grounds for possession, which will be approximately the same as those for the assured tenancy (see below).
- A notice requiring possession at the end of the term is usually served two months before that date.
- A notice must be served before any rent increase giving one months clear notice and providing details of the rent increase.

If the landlord wishes to get possession of his/her property, in this case before the expiry of the contractual term, the landlord has to gain a court order. A notice of seeking possession must be served, giving fourteen days notice and following similar grounds of possession as an assured tenancy.

The landlord cannot simply tell a tenant to leave before the end of the agreed term.

If the tenancy runs on after the end of the fixed term then the landlord can regain possession by giving the required two months notice, as mentioned above.

At the end of the term for which the assured shorthold tenancy has been granted, the landlord has an automatic right to possession.

An assured shorthold tenancy will become periodic (will run from week to week) when the initial term of six months has elapsed and the landlord has not brought the tenancy to an end. A periodic tenancy is brought to an end with two months notice.

Assured shorthold tenants can be evicted only on certain grounds, some discretionary, some mandatory (see below).

In order for the landlord of an assured shorthold tenant to regain possession of the property, a notice of seeking possession (of property) must be served, giving fourteen days notice of expiry and stating the ground for possession. A copy of this notice is shown in Appendix 2. This notice is similar to a notice to quit, discussed in the previous chapter.

Following the fourteen days a court order must be obtained. Although gaining a court order is not complicated, a solicitor will usually be used. Court costs can be awarded against the tenant.

Security of tenure: The ways in which a tenant can lose their home as an assured shorthold tenant

There are a number of circumstances called grounds (mandatory and discretionary) whereby a landlord can start a court action to evict a tenant.

The following are the *mandatory* grounds (where the judge must give the landlord possession) and *discretionary* grounds (where the judge does not have to give the landlord possession) on which a court can order possession if the home is subject to an assured tenancy.

The mandatory grounds for possession of a property let on an assured (shorthold) tenancy

There are eight mandatory grounds for possession, which, if proved, leave the court with no choice but to make an order for possession. It is very important that you understand these.

Ground One is used where the landlord has served a notice, no later than at the beginning of the tenancy, warning the tenant that this ground may be used against him/her.

This ground is used where the landlord wishes to recover the property as his or her principal (first and only) home or the spouse's (wife's or husbands) principal home. ***The ground is not available to a person who bought the premises for gain (profit) whilst they were occupied.***

Ground Two is available where the property is subject to a mortgage and if the landlord does not pay the mortgage, could lose the home.

Grounds Three and Four relate to holiday lettings.

Ground Five is a special one, applicable to ministers of religion.

Ground Six relates to the demolition or reconstruction of the property.

Ground Seven applies if a tenant dies and in his will leaves the tenancy to someone else: but the landlord must start proceedings against the new tenant within a year of the death if he wants to evict the new tenant.

Ground Eight concerns rent arrears. This ground applies if, both at the date of the serving of the notice seeking possession and at the date of the hearing of the action, the rent is at least 8 weeks in arrears or two months in arrears. This is the main ground used by landlords when rent is not being paid.

The discretionary grounds for possession of a property, which is let on an assured tenancy

As we have seen, the discretionary grounds for possession are those in relation to which the court has some powers over whether or not the landlord can evict. In other words, the final decision is left to the judge. Often the judge will prefer to grant a suspended order first, unless the circumstances are dramatic.

Ground Nine applies when suitable alternative accommodation is available or will be when the possession order takes effect. As we have seen, if the landlord wishes to obtain possession of his or her property in order to use it for other purposes then suitable alternative accommodation has to be provided.

Ground Ten deals with rent arrears as does *ground eleven*. These grounds are distinct from the mandatory grounds, as there does not have to be a fixed arrear in terms of time scale, e.g., 8 weeks. The judge, therefore, has some choice as to whether or not to evict. In practice, this ground will not be relevant to managers of assured shorthold tenancies.

Ground Twelve concerns any broken obligation of the tenancy. As we have seen with the protected tenancy, there are a number of conditions of the tenancy agreement, such as the requirement not to racially or sexually harass a neighbor. Ground Twelve will be used if these conditions are broken.

Ground Thirteen deals with the deterioration of the dwelling as a result of a tenant's neglect. This is connected with the structure of the property and is the same as for a protected tenancy. It puts the responsibility on the tenant to look after the premises.

Ground Fourteen concerns nuisance, annoyance and illegal or immoral use. This is where a tenant or anyone connected with the tenant has caused a nuisance to neighbors.

Ground 14A this ground deals with domestic violence.

Ground 15 concerns the condition of the furniture and tenants neglect. As Ground thirteen puts some responsibility on the tenant to look after the structure of the building so Ground Fifteen makes the tenant responsible for the furniture and fittings.

Ground 16 covers former employees. The premises were let to a former tenant by a landlord seeking possession and the tenant has ceased to be in that employment.

Ground 17 is where a person or that persons agents makes a false or reckless statement and this has caused the landlord to grant the tenancy under false pretences.

The description of the grounds above is intended as a guide only. For a fuller description please refer to the 1988 Housing Act, section 7, Schedule two,) as amended by the 1996 Housing Act) which is available at reference libraries.

Fast track possession

In November 1993, following changes to the County Court Rules, a facility was introduced which enabled landlords of tenants with assured shorthold tenancies to apply for possession of their property without the usual time delay involved in waiting for a court date and attendance at court. This is known as "fast track possession" It cannot be used for rent arrears or other grounds. It is used to gain possession of a property when the fixed term of six months or more has come to an end and the tenant will not move.

Payment of rent

If the landlord wishes to raise rent, at least one month's minimum notice must be given. The rent cannot be raised more than once for the same tenant in one year. Tenants have the right to challenge a rent increase if they think it is unfair by referring the rent to a Rent Assessment Committee. The committee will prevent the landlord from raising the rent above the ordinary market rent for that type of property. We will be discussing rent and rent control further on in this book.

6

JOINT TENANCIES

Joint tenancies: the position of two or more people who have a tenancy agreement for one property

Although it is the normal state of affairs for a tenancy agreement to be granted to one person, this is not always the case.

A tenancy can also be granted to two or more people and is then known as a *joint tenancy*. The position of joint tenants is exactly the same as that of single tenants. In other words, there is still one tenancy even though it is shared.

Each tenant is responsible for paying the rent and observing the terms and conditions of the tenancy agreement. No one joint tenant can prevent another joint tenant's access to the premises.

If one of the joint tenants dies then his or her interest will automatically pass to the remaining joint tenants. A joint tenant cannot dispose of his or her interest in a will.

If one joint tenant, however, serves a notice to quit (notice to leave the property) on another joint tenant(s) then the tenancy will come to an end and the landlord can apply to court for a possession order, if the remaining tenant does not leave.

The position of a wife or husband in relation to joint tenancies is rather more complex because the married person has more rights when it comes to the home than the single person.

Remember: the position of a tenant who has signed a joint tenancy agreement is exactly the same as that of the single tenant. If one person leaves, the other(s) have the responsibilities of the tenancy. If one person leaves without paying his share of the rent then the other tenants will have to pay instead.

7

RENT AND OTHER CHARGES

The payment of rent and other financial matters

If a tenancy is protected under the Rent Act 1977, as described earlier there is the right to apply to the Rent Officer for the setting of a fair rent for the property.

The assured tenant

The assured tenant has far fewer rights in relation to rent control than the protected tenant.

The Housing Act 1988 allows a landlord to charge whatever he likes. There is no right to a fair or reasonable rent with an assured tenancy. If the tenancy is assured then there will usually be a formula in the tenancy which will provide guidance for rent increases. If not then the landlord can set what rent he or she likes within reason. If the amount is unreasonable then the tenant can refer the matter to the rent assessment committee. The rent can sometimes be negotiated at the outset of the tenancy. This rent has to be paid as long as the contractual term of the tenancy lasts. Once the contractual term has expired, the landlord is entitled to continue to charge the same rent.

On expiry of an assured shorthold the landlord is free to grant a new tenancy and set the rent to a level that is compatible with the market.

Rent control for assured shorthold tenants

We have seen that the assured shorthold tenancy is for a minimum period of six months. Like the assured tenant, the assured shorthold tenant has no right to request that a fair rent should be set. The rent is a market rent.

As with an assured tenancy, the assured shorthold tenant has the right to appeal to a Rent Assessment Committee in the case of what he/she considers an unreasonable rent. This may be done during the contractual term of the tenancy. The Committee will consider whether the rent is significantly higher than is usual for a similar property.

If the Committee assesses a different rent from that set by the landlord, they may set a date when the increase will take effect. The rent cannot be backdated to before the date of the application. Once a decision has been reached by the Committee, the landlord cannot increase the rent for at least twelve months, or on termination of the tenancy. Details of the local Rent Assessment Committee can be obtained from the Rent Officer Service at your local authority.

Housing benefit and local housing allowance

If you are renting a property or a room from a private landlord, the Local Housing Allowance is used to work out how much housing benefit is payable. The Local Housing Allowance was introduced on 7th April 2008. Those claiming before that will not be affected unless they have changed address or had a break in their claim.

With the local housing allowance, housing benefit is worked out according to where the property is and who is living in the property. Allowances are set for different types of accommodation in each area. The rates range from a single room in a shared house to properties with five bedrooms.

Local Housing Allowance rates are calculated each month for individual areas, known as Broad Market Rental Areas. The Local Housing Allowance rate for each property size is based on the 'middle of the range' rental figure for the area. Exactly half of the rental properties of that size in the area will be affordable if you claim Housing benefit under the Local Housing Allowance rules.

Where the rates are published

Local Housing Allowance rates are published at the end of each month for the following month and can be checked with the local authority direct or via their website.

How much is payable

Housing benefit will be based on the Local Housing Allowance rate that applies to the individual. If the rent is lower than the Local Authority Allowance Rate, an individual can keep any excess up to a maximum of

£15 per week. If the rent is higher than the Local Housing Allowance Rate then the tenant has to make up the difference or look for alternative accommodation.

Council tax and the tenant

Council tax is based on property values, and not individual people. This means that there is one bill for each individual dwelling, rather than separate bills for each person. The number and type of people who live in the dwelling may affect the size of the final bill. A discount of 25% is given for people who live alone. Each property is placed in a valuation band with different properties paying more or less depending on their individual value. Tenants who feel that their home has been placed in the wrong valuation band can appeal to their local authority council tax department.

Who has to pay the council tax?

In most cases the tenant occupying the dwelling will have to pay the council tax. However, a landlord will be responsible for paying the council tax where there are several households living in one dwelling. This will usually be hostels, bed-sits and other non self-contained flats where people share things such as cooking and washing facilities. The council tax on this type of property remains the responsibility of the landlord even if all but one of the tenants move out. Although the landlord has the responsibility for paying the council tax, he/she will normally try to pass on the increased cost through rents. However, as we have seen, there is a set procedure for a landlord to follow if he/she wishes to increase rent.

Dwellings which are exempt

Certain properties will be exempt from the council tax, such as student's halls of residences and nurse's homes. Properties with all students resident will be exempt from the tax. However, if one non-student moves in then that property will no longer be exempt from tax. Uninhabitable empty properties are exempt from tax, as they are not counted as dwellings.

This is not the same as homes, which have been declared as unfit for human habitation by Environmental Health officers. The deciding factor will be whether or not a property is capable of being lived in.

Reductions in council tax bills

Tenants in self-contained accommodation who live alone will be entitled to a discount of 25% of the total bill. Tenants may also qualify for the discount if they share their homes with people who do not count for council tax purposes. Such people are: children under eighteen; students; patients resident in hospital; people who are severely mentally impaired; low paid care workers; eighteen or nineteen year olds still at school (or just left); people in prison (except for non-payment of fines or the council tax); and people caring for someone with a disability who is not a spouse, partner or child under eighteen.

Council tax benefits available for those on low income

Tenants on very low income, except for students, will usually be able to claim council tax benefit. This can cover up to 100% of the council tax.

Tenants with disabilities may be entitled to further discounts. Tenants who are not responsible for individual council tax, but pay it through their rent, can claim housing benefit to cover the increase.

The rules covering council tax liability can be obtained from a Citizens Advice Bureau or from your local authority council tax department.

Service charges

A service charge covers provision of services other than those covered by the rent. A rental payment will normally cover maintenance charges, loan charges if any, and also profit. Other services, such as cleaning and gardening, will be covered by a separate charge, known as a service charge. A *registered* rent reflects the cost of any services provided by the landlord. An assured rent set by a landlord will normally include services, which must be outlined in the agreement.

The fact that the charges are variable must be written into a tenancy agreement and the landlord has a legal duty to provide the tenant with annual budgets and accounts and has to consult when he or she wishes to spend over a certain amount of money, currently £250 per dwelling or £100 for contracts such as cleaning and lift maintenance if they are for more than 12 months.

The form of consultation, which must take place, is that of writing to all those affected and informing them of:

-The landlord's intention to carry out work;

-Why these works are seen to be necessary;

This first notice is for 30 days after which another notice must be sent containing:

-The estimated cost of the works;
-At least two estimates or inviting residents to see two estimates.

A period of twenty-eight days must be allowed before work is carried out. This gives time for any feedback from tenants.

The landlord can incur reasonable expense, without consultation, if the work is deemed to be necessary, i.e. emergency works.

If a service charge is variable then a landlord has certain legal obligations, which are clearly laid out in the 1985 and 1987 Landlord and Tenant Acts as amended by the 2002 Commonhold and Leasehold Reform Act.

8

THE RIGHT TO QUIET ENJOYMENT OF A HOME

Earlier, we saw that when a tenancy agreement is signed, the landlord is contracting to give quiet enjoyment of the tenant's home. This means that they have the right to live peacefully in the home without harassment.

The landlord is obliged not to do anything that will disturb the right to the quiet enjoyment of the home. The most serious breach of this right would be for the landlord to wrongfully evict a tenant.

Eviction: what can be done against unlawful harassment and eviction

It is a criminal offence for a landlord unlawfully to evict a residential occupier (whether or not a tenant!). The occupier has protection under the Protection from Eviction Act 1977 section 1(2).

If the tenant or occupier is unlawfully evicted his/her first course should be to seek an injunction compelling the landlord to readmit him/her to the premises. It is an unfortunate fact but many landlords will attempt to evict tenants forcefully. In doing so they break the law.

However, the landlord may, on termination of the tenancy recover possession without a court order if the agreement was entered into after 15th January 1989 and it falls into one of the following six situations:

- The occupier shares any accommodation with the landlord and the landlord occupies the premises as his or her only or principal home.
- The occupier shares any of the accommodation with a member of the landlords family, that person occupies the premises as their only or principal home, and the landlord occupies as his or her only or principal home premises in the same building.
- The tenancy or license was granted temporarily to an occupier

who entered the premises as a trespasser.

- The tenancy or license gives the right to occupy for the purposes of a holiday.
- The tenancy or license is rent-free.
- The license relates to occupation of a hostel.

There is also a section in the 1977 Protection from Eviction Act which provides a defense for otherwise unlawful eviction and that is that the landlord may repossess if it is thought that the tenant no longer lives on the premises. It is important to note that, in order for such action to be seen as a crime under the 1977 Protection from Eviction Act, the intention of the landlord to evict must be proved.

However, there is another offence, namely harassment, which also needs to be proved. Even if the landlord is not guilty of permanently depriving a tenant of their home he/she could be guilty of harassment.

Such actions as cutting off services, deliberately allowing the premises to fall into a state of disrepair, or even forcing unwanted sexual attentions, all constitute harassment and a breach of the right to *quiet enjoyment*.

The 1977 Protection from Eviction Act also prohibits the use of violence to gain entry to premises. Even in situations where the landlord has the right to gain entry without a court order it is an offence to use violence.

If entry to the premises is opposed then the landlord should gain a court order.

What can be done against unlawful evictions?

There are two main remedies for unlawful eviction: damages and, as stated above, an injunction.

The injunction

An injunction is an order from the court requiring a person to do, or not to do something. In the case of eviction the court can grant an injunction requiring the landlord to allow a tenant back into occupation of the premises. In the case of harassment an order can be made preventing the landlord from harassing the tenant.

Failure to comply with an injunction is contempt of court and can result in a fine or imprisonment.

Damages

In some cases the tenant can press for *financial compensation* following unlawful eviction. Financial compensation may have to be paid in cases where financial loss has occurred or in cases where personal hardship alone has occurred.

The tenant can also press for *special damages,* which means that the tenant may recover the definable out-of-pocket expenses. These could be expenses arising as a result of having to stay in a hotel because of the eviction. Receipts must be kept in that case. There are also *general damages*, which can be awarded in compensation for stress, suffering and inconvenience.

A tenant may also seek *exemplary damages* where it can be proved that the landlord has disregarded the law deliberately with the intention of making a profit out of the displacement of the tenant.

9

REPAIRS AND IMPROVEMENTS

Repairs and improvements generally: the landlord and tenants obligations

Repairs are essential works to keep the property in good order. Improvements are alterations to the property, e.g. the installation of a shower.

As we have seen, some tenancies are periodic, week-to-week or month-to-month. If a tenancy falls into this category, or is a fixed-term tenancy for less than seven years, and began after October 1961, then a landlord is legally responsible for most major repairs to the flat or house. Repairs are paid for out of a tenants rent.

If a tenancy began after 15th January 1989 then, in addition to the above responsibility, the landlord is also responsible for repairs to common parts and service fittings.

The area of law dealing with the landlord and tenants repairing obligations is the 1985 Landlord and Tenant Act, section 11.

This section of the Act is known as a covenant and cannot be excluded by informal agreement between landlord and tenant. In other words the landlord is legally responsible whether he or she likes it or not. Parties to a tenancy, however, may make an application to a court mutually to vary or exclude this section.

An example of repairs a landlord is responsible for:

Leaking roofs and guttering;
Rotting windows;
Rising damp;
Damp walls;
Faulty electrical wiring;
Dangerous ceilings and staircases;
Faulty gas and water pipes;
Broken water heaters and boilers;
Broken lavatories, sinks or baths.

In shared housing the landlord must see that shared halls, stairways, kitchens and bathrooms are maintained and kept clean and lit.

Normally, tenants are responsible only for minor repairs, e.g., broken door handles, cupboard doors, etc. Tenants will also be responsible for decorations unless they have been damaged as a result of the landlord's failure to do repair.

A landlord will be responsible for repairs only if the repair has been reported. It is therefore important to report repairs in writing and keep a copy. If the repair is not carried out then action can be taken. Damages can also be claimed.

Compensation can be claimed, with the appropriate amount being the reduction in the value of the premises to the tenant caused by the landlord's failure to repair. If the tenant carries out the repairs then the amount expended will represent the decrease in value.

The tenant does not have the right to withhold rent because of a breach of repairing covenant by the landlord. However, depending on the repair, the landlord will not have a very strong case in court if rent is withheld.

REPORTING REPAIRS TO A LANDLORD

The tenant has to tell the landlord or the person collecting the rent straight away when a repair needs doing. It is advisable that it is in writing, listing the repairs that need to be done.

Once a tenant has reported a repair the landlord must do it within a reasonable period of time. What is reasonable will depend on the nature of the repair. If certain emergency work needs to be done by the council, such as leaking guttering or drains a notice can be served ordering the landlord to do the work within a short time. In exceptional cases if a home cannot be made habitable at reasonable cost the council may declare that the house must no longer be used, in which case the council has a legal duty to re-house a tenant.

If after the council has served notice the landlord still does not do the work, the council can send in its own builder or, in some cases take the landlord to court. A tenant must allow a landlord access to do repairs. The landlord has to give twenty-four hours notice of wishing to gain access.

The tenants rights whilst repairs are being carried out

The landlord must ensure that the repairs are done in an orderly and efficient way with minimum inconvenience to the tenant If the works are disruptive or if property or decorations are damaged the tenant can apply to the court for compensation or, if necessary, for an order to make the landlord behave reasonably.

If the landlord genuinely needs the house empty to do the work he/she can ask the tenant to vacate it and can if necessary get a court order against the tenant.

A *written agreement* should be drawn up making it clear that the tenant can move back in when the repairs are completed and stating what the arrangements for fuel charges and rent are.

If a person is an *assured* tenant the landlord could get a court order to make that person give up the home permanently if there is work to be done with him/her in occupation in occupation.

Can the landlord put the rent up after doing repairs?
If there is a service charge for maintenance, the landlord may be able to pass on the cost of the work(s).

Tenants rights to make improvements to a property
Unlike carrying out repairs the tenant will not normally have the right to insist that the landlord make actual alterations to the home. However, a tenant needs the following amenities and the law states that you should have them:

- Bath or shower;

- Wash hand basin; Hot and cold water at each bath, basin or shower;

- an indoor toilet.

If these amenities do not exist then the tenant can contact the council's Environmental Health Officer. An improvement notice can be served on the landlord ordering him to put the amenity in.

Disabled tenants
If a tenant is disabled he/she may need special items of equipment in the accommodation. The local authority may help in providing and,

occasionally, paying for these. The tenant will need to obtain the permission of the landlord. If you require more information then contact the social services department locally.

Shared housing. The position of tenants in shared houses (Houses in Multiple Occupation)

Houses in Multiple Occupation

A major change to improve standards of shared housing was introduced in 2006. The parts of the Housing Act 2004 relating to the licensing of HMO's (Houses in Multiple Occupation) and the new Health and Safety rating System for assessing property conditions came into effect on 6th April 2006.

The Act requires landlords of many HMO's to apply for licences. The HMO's that need to be licensed are those with:

- Three or more storeys, which are
- Occupied by five or more people forming two or more households (i.e. people not related, living together as a couple etc) and
- Which have an element of shared facilities (eg kitchen, bathroom etc)

As far as licensing is concerned, attics and basements are included as storeys if they are used as living accommodation. Previously, HMO's were only defined as houses converted into flats or bedsits, but the new Act widens this definition and many more types of shared houses are now included.

A local authority will have a list of designated properties will have a list of those properties which are designated HMO's and they will need to be licensed.

Usually, landlords will need to apply to a local authority private sector unit for licences. It has been illegal for landlords to manage designated properties without a licence since July 2006.

Landlords will have to complete an application form and pay a fee, the local authority will then assess whether the property is suitable for the number of people the landlord wants to rent it to. In most case, the local authority, their agents, will visit a property to assess facilities and also fire precautions. A decision will then be taken to grant a license.

There is a fee for registration, councils set the fee and the ones shown below are indicative of a southern local authority:

- Shared houses-five sharers landlords first house £640
- Subsequent house £590
- Plus £10 each additional occupier over five

Hostels

- 10 occupiers £690
- 20 occupiers £790
- 50 occupiers £1100
- 75 occupiers £1340

Sanitation health and hygiene

Local authorities have a duty to serve an owner with a notice requiring the provision of WCs when a property has insufficient sanitation, sanitation meaning toilet waste disposal. They will also serve notice if it is thought that the existing sanitation is inadequate and is harmful to health or is a nuisance. Local authorities have similar powers under various Public Health Acts to require owners to put right bad drains and sewers, also food storage facilities and vermin, plus the containing of disease.

The Environmental Health Department, if it considers the problem bad enough will serve a notice requiring the landlord to put the defect right. In certain cases the local authority can actually do the work and require the landlord to pay for it. This is called work *in default*.

Housing Grants

There are a range of grants and loans available, almost all discretionary and means tested for help and assistance with property improvement.

These will change from time to time and checks should be made with the local authority.

Disabled Facilities Grant

The only mandatory grant is the Disabled Facilities Grant, given to those in need, which has been assessed by an Occupational Therapist, the grant has a ceiling. Information of which can be obtained from the local authority. Has the name suggests it is for those who are disabled and are n need of works which will make there property accessible and usable for disabled people.

Apart fro Disabled Facilities Grant, a local authority can offer different types of help with home improvements. Local authorities, generally, can give help to:

- Adapt, improve or repair a home. This can be in the form of a grant or loan or could be by way of supplying labour pr materials.
- Buy a new home if it decides that it would be a better way of improving a person's living conditions. This help could be by way of grant or loan.
- Buy your current home.
- Demolish your home, if this is seen as the best way forward.

All local authorities will have written material regarding grants and loans, plus other help available.

Energy Innovation Grants

These grants are subject to the availability of funding and are related to the policy of the local authority.

10

WHAT SHOULD BE PROVIDED UNDER THE TENANCY

Furniture

A landlords decision whether or not to furnish property will depend on the sort of tenant that he is aiming to find. The actual legal distinction between a furnished property and an unfurnished property has faded into insignificance.

If a landlord does let a property as furnished then the following would be the absolute minimum:

- Seating, such as sofa and armchair

- Cabinet or sideboard

- Kitchen tables and chairs

- Cooker and refrigerator

- Bedroom furniture

Even unfurnished lets, however, are expected to come complete with a basic standard of furniture, particularly carpets and kitchen goods. If the landlord does supply electrical equipment then he or she is able to disclaim any repairing responsibility for it, but this must be mentioned in the tenancy agreement.

Services

Usually, a landlord will only provide services to a tenant if the property is a flat situated in a block or is a house on a private estate. The services will include cyclical painting and maintenance, usually on a three to four year basis (flats) and gardening and cleaning plus repairs to the communal areas, plus communal electricity bills and water rates. These services should be outlined in the agreement and are administered within a strict framework of law, The 1985 Landlord and Tenant Act Section 18-30 as amended by the 1987 LTA and the 2002 Commonhold and Leasehold Reform Act. The landlord has rigid duties imposed within this Act, such as the need to gain estimates before commencing works and also to consult with residents where the cost exceeds £250 per flat or £100 for works based on an annual contract such as lift maintenance, gardening etc.. The landlord must give the tenant four weeks notice of intention to carry out works inviting feedback then a further four weeks notice with estimates.

Tenants have the right to see audited accounts and invoices relating to work. Service charges, as an extra payment over and above the rent are always contentious and it is an area that Landlords need to be aware of if they are to manage professionally.

Repairs
See chapter on repairing obligations

Insurance
Strictly speaking, there is no duty on either landlord or tenant to insure the property. However, it is highly advisable for the landlord to provide buildings insurance as he/she stands to lose a lot more in the event of fire or other disaster than the tenant. A landlord letting property for a first time would be well advised to consult his/ her insurance company before letting as there are different criteria to observe when a property is let and not to inform the company could invalidate the policy.

At the end of the tenancy
The tenancy agreement will normally spell out the obligations of the tenant at the end of the term. Essentially, the tenant will have an obligation to:

- have kept the interior clean and tidy and in a good state of repair and decoration
- have not caused any damage
- have replaced anything that they have broken
- replace or pay for the repair of anything that they have damaged
- pay for the laundering of the linen

- pay for any other laundering
- put anything that they have moved or removed back to how it was

Sometimes a tenancy agreement will make provision for the tenants paying for anything that is soiled at their own expense, although sensible wear and tear is allowed for.

The landlord will normally be able to recover any loss from the deposit that the tenant has given on entering the premises (see section on Deposit Protection Scheme). However, sometimes, the tenants will withhold rent for the last month in order to recoup their deposit. It is up to the landlord to negotiate re-imbursement for any damage caused, but this should be within reason. There is a remedy, which can be pursued in the Small Claims court if the tenants refuse to pay but this is rarely successful.

11

GOING TO COURT TO REGAIN POSSESSION OF A HOME

There may come a time when the landlord needs to go to court to regain possession of his property. This will usually arise when the contract has been breached by the tenant, for non-payment of rent or for some other breach such as nuisance or harassment. As we have seen, a tenancy can be brought to an end in a court on one of the grounds for possession. However, as the tenancy will usually be an assured shorthold then it is necessary to consider whether you are in a position to be given two months notice, as opposed to going to court.

If the landlord decides, for whatever reasons, to go to court, then any move to regain a property for breach of agreement will commence in the county court in the area in which the property is. The first steps in ending the tenancy will necessitate the serving of a notice of seeking possession using one of the Grounds for Possession detailed earlier in the book. If the tenancy is protected then 28 days must be given, the notice must be in prescribed form and served on the tenant personally. See appendix for sample notice seeking possession.

If the tenancy is assured shorthold, which is usually always the case now, then 14 days notice of seeking possession can be used. In all cases the ground to be relied upon must be clearly outlined in the notice.

If the case is more complex, then this will entail a particulars of claim being prepared, usually by a solicitor, as opposed to a standard possession form.

A fee is paid when sending the particulars to court, which is currently £150 if the claim is initiated in the county court and £100 if using Possession Claims Online (PCOL). PCOL can only be used if the possession is also for rent or mortgage arrears.

The standard form which the landlord uses for routine rent arrears cases is called the N5 and there will be an accompanying Particulars of Claim. Both of these forms can be obtained from the court. When completed, the forms should be sent in duplicate to the county court and a copy retained for you. The court will send a copy of the Particulars of claim and the summons to the tenant. They will send a form which gives the landlord a case number and court date to appear, known as the return date.

On the return date, if you are defending yourself you should arrive at court at least 15 minutes early. You can represent yourself in simple cases but are advised to use a solicitor for more contentious cases.

A number of orders are available. However, if the landlord has gone to court on the mandatory ground eight then if the fact is proved then he will get possession immediately. If not, then the judge can grant an order, suspended whilst the tenant finds time to pay.

Whatever the order, a bailiff's warrant will be needed to finally evict the tenant from the property. This can be obtained after the order is given by filling in the appropriate form and paying a fee to the bailiff office.

In a lot of cases, it is more expedient for a landlord to serve notice-requiring possession, if the tenancy has reached the end of the period, and then wait two months before the property is regained. This saves the cost and time of going to court particularly if the ground is one of nuisance or other, which will involve solicitors.

If a tenancy has reached the end of the contractual term and the landlord wish's to recover his property then a "fast track" procedure is available which entails gaining an order for possession and bailiff's order by post. This can be used in cases with the exception of rent arrears.

12

PUBLIC SECTOR TENANCIES

Lettings of property by local authorities are specifically excluded from being assured tenancies under the 1988 Housing Act or protected tenancies under the 1977 Rent Act. Some Housing Associations with older tenancies also have this restriction.

Tenancies signed by Local authority tenants are known as *secure* tenancies and are protected by the 1985 Housing Act.

Secure Tenancies

Secure tenants have security of tenure under the 1985 Housing Act. This means that they cannot be evicted without a court order. However, security can be lost if the following circumstances arise:

- A tenant ceases to use the home as his/her only or principal home. This means that the property let under a secure tenancy should be lived in 80% of the time
- If a property is sub-let without permission then security is lost
- If a property is abandoned then security is lost unless the tenant can demonstrate a clear intention to return.

A secure tenant has many rights over and above those of an assured tenant. There is the right to buy a property, the right to mutually exchange with someone else, the right to sub-let with permission and the right to succeed to a tenancy on death or by assignment.

Right-to-buy.

Perhaps the most valuable right enjoyed by a secure tenant is the right to buy either the freehold, in the case of a house, or the leasehold, in the case of a flat. In order to claim this right there is also a residence qualification to fulfill. The tenant, or the tenant's spouse must have been resident as a secure tenant (not necessarily in the same property) for five years prior to the application to buy. This doesn't have to be five consecutive years. The price of the property will be subject to a substantial discount in recognition of the length of time that the tenant has been resident there and also will be dependant on regions. The maximum discounts currently applicable in 2010 are as follows

- £16,000 in Wales
- £16,000 in London (Unless your home is in Barking, Dagenham or Havering where the maximum discount is £38,000
- £22,000 in the North East of England
- £24,000 in the East Midlands, Yorkshire and Humber
- £26,000 in the North West of England and the Midlands
- £30,000 in the South West of England
- £34,000 in the east of England (Unless in Watford where the maximum is £16,000).

In the South East of England the maximum discount is £38,000, unless the home is in certain areas where it will be £16,000. This should always be checked with the local authority in your area. There may be other factors that affect the discount, such as the 'cost floor' rule where the landlord has spent more on the property over the last ten years than it's current worth.

If the property is sold within five years of purchase then the discount will have to be repaid on a sliding level-all the discount if sold within the first year of purchase, 80% in the second year and so on.

If the property is sold within ten years of purchase then you must first offer it to your old landlord, e.g. the council or housing association, or another social landlord in the area.

Right to Buy and third party agreements

Discount will also have to be repaid if there is an agreement to transfer the property to a private landlord or company within five years. The amount to be paid back will depend on the transfer. If the agreement is signed before the sale is completed then all the discount will have to be paid back.

Rights to succeed to a secure tenancy

The tenancy does not end with the death of a secure tenant. If there is a spouse then he/she will succeed to the tenancy subject to having been resident for 1 year, occupying as an only or principal home, prior to the application to succeed.

The courts have held that only persons of the opposite sex can be defined as spouse. However, this ruling may certainly be challenged in the European Court of Human Rights.

Where there is no spouse as defined then a member of the family can succeed, again with the residence qualification in place. If a family cannot decide who should succeed then the local authority or body granting the secure tenancy can make a final decision.

Only one succession is allowed and, on the death of the successor, the local authority can terminate the tenancy through formal procedures and re-let to whom it wishes.

Right to repair and to make improvements

Secure tenants have a right to carry out their own repairs, to make improvements, subject to the landlords consent and also the right to compensation if repairs are not carried out within a set timescale.

In general, a secure tenancy is a stronger form of tenure than an assured tenancy. Although housing associations grant secure tenancies in certain circumstances, in the main these tenancies are only granted by Local Authorities.

A secure tenancy, like an assured tenancy, can only be brought to an end by a court. There are 17 Grounds for possession in the 1985 Housing Act as amended by the 1996 Housing Act. However, unlike the assured tenancy, where 8 grounds are mandatory, all 17 grounds in the secure tenancy are discretionary. Many of these grounds reflect the grounds in the 1988 Housing Act. For a tenancy to be brought to an end, a notice of seeking possession must be served and an application to court made, in the same way as with an assured tenant.

Introductory tenancies

The 1996 Housing Act allowed local housing authorities to elect to set up an introductory tenancy scheme – an election that can be revoked at any time. If the local authority has decided to embark on the policy of adopting introductory tenancies then any tenancy that would be otherwise secure will be an introductory tenancy for a period of one year. In effect this is a period of probation and was introduced to tighten up on the overall behaviour of some of the worst offenders who take up local authority tenancies.

Demoted tenancies

Another form of tenancy, which is applicable to both councils and housing associations is the Demoted Tenancy. This was introduced by the Anti-Social Behavior Act 2003 and enables local authorities and housing associations to deal more effectively with anti-social tenants. A landlord must go to court to seek demotion and, if successful, the tenancy will become non-secure and it will be that much easier for the landlord to gain possession.

Housing Association tenants

Housing associations are now one of the major providers of affordable housing in the country. Many housing associations are registered with the Tenants Services Authority, and are known as Registered Social Landlords (RSL's). In order to receive public funding, a housing association has to be registered as an RSL.

Many housing associations now grant a variety of tenancies, assured, assured shorthold, licenses and also develop leasehold property. The relevant housing acts will apply to these tenancy types. However, because of the TSA's monitoring and regulatory function, the assured tenancy issued by a housing association will be significantly stronger than assured tenancies in the private sector.

All tenancies granted after January 15th 1989, by housing associations, will be assured tenancies. Those granted before will be secure tenancies. If a secure tenant transfers to a property occupied by an assured tenant they will lose their secure tenancy. Likewise, the person transferring into a secure tenancy will take on that tenancy.

The assured tenant of a housing association has much the same rights of a secure tenant, passed to them contractually as a result of the TSA's Tenants Charter. The only exceptions are the right to buy and a difference in how rents are set.

Many housing associations have, since 1988 taken transfer of local authority property. These large-scale 'stock transfers' have resulted in local authorities housing powers being diminished and those of housing associations enhanced. In cases of stock transfer, the tenancy agreements of local authority tenants will become assured but with a preserved right to buy.

13

PRIVATE TENANCIES IN SCOTLAND

The law governing the relationship between private landlords and tenants in Scotland is different to that in England. Since the beginning of 1989, new private sector tenancies in Scotland have been covered by the Housing (Scotland) Act 1988. Following the passage of this Act, private sector tenants no longer have any protection as far as rent levels are concerned and tenants enjoy less security of tenure.

There are four essential elements in the creation of a tenancy under Scottish law:

- An agreement between landlord and tenant
- The payment of rent. If someone is allowed to occupy a property without an agreement then this will not amount to a tenancy
- A fixed permission date (called an 'ish')
- Possession

The agreement must be in writing if the tenancy is for a period of 1 year or more. Agreements of less than a year can be oral.

Protected tenancies

Before 1989, most private sector tenancies were likely to be protected tenancies. A protected tenancy is a contractual tenancy covered by the Rent Act (Scotland) 1984 and must satisfy the following requirements:

- The house must be let as a dwelling house (this can apply to a house or part of a house)
- The house must be a separate dwelling
- The ratable value must be less than a specified sum

Various categories of dwellings did not qualify as protected tenancies. A protected tenancy retains its status until the death of a tenant or his or her spouse, or any eligible successor, and therefore some protected tenancies are still in existence today.

Grounds for possession

As is the case in England and Wales, where there is no protected tenancy, the landlord may possess a property only by obtaining a court order. The landlord must serve a notice to quit, giving 28 days notice. A ground for possession must be shown, either discretionary or mandatory before possession can be given.

The grounds for possession are similar to those in England and Wales, with ten mandatory and ten discretionary grounds applying.

Fair rent system

A fair rent system, similar to England and Wales, exists in Scotland for protected tenants. There is a set procedure to be followed, with either the landlord or tenant, or jointly, making an application to the rent officer. Once fixed, the rent is valid for three years. A fresh application can be made within three years if circumstances relating to the tenancy radically alter, such as a substantial refurbishment.

Assured tenants

Under the Housing (Scotland) Act 1988, the assured tenancy was introduced into Scotland coming into force after 2nd January 1989. This is very similar indeed to the assured tenancy introduced into England and Wales in 1989.

A Scottish assured tenancy has three elements:

- the tenancy must be of a house or flat or self contained dwelling. For an agreement to exist, there must be an agreement, rent payable a termination date and possession, as there is in all leases in Scotland
- The house must be let as a separate dwelling. A tenancy may be of a flat, part of a house, or even a single room, provided it is possible for the tenant to carry on all 'the major activities of residential life there, i.e. sleeping, cooking and feeding'.
- The tenant must be an individual. A company cannot be given an assured tenancy

The list of exclusions from assured tenancy status are the same as those in England and all the other provisions concerning rent, sub-letting succession, security of tenure and so on, apply.

The grounds for possession and the law governing termination of tenancies is a reflection of English Law.

Short assured tenancies

The Housing Act (Scotland) also introduced 'short assured tenancies', a distinct form of assured tenancy for a fixed term of six months. Again, this is a reflection of the assured shorthold with the same provisions applying.

14

OWNER OCCUPATION-GENERAL CONSIDERATIONS WHEN BUYING A HOUSE OR FLAT

Budget

Before beginning to look for a house you need to sit down and give careful thought to the costs involved in the whole process. The starting point is to identify the different areas in the overall transaction.

Deposit

Sometimes the estate agent will ask you for a small deposit when you make the offer (see Estate Agents, Chapter 2 and 15). This indicates that you are serious about the offer and is a widespread and legitimate practice, as long as the deposit is not too much, £100 is usual.

The main deposit for the property, i.e., the difference between the mortgage and what has been accepted for the property, isn't paid until the exchange of contracts. Once you have exchanged contracts on a property the purchase is legally binding. Until then, you are free to withdraw. The deposit cannot be reclaimed after exchange.

Banks will normally lend up to 95% of the purchase price of the property. However, the less you borrow, the more favourable terms you can normally get from bank or building society.

Stamp duty

Stamp duty is a tax paid on purchase of property. Currently the tax is as follows:

- o Up to £125,000 Nil duty (£250,000 for first time buyers following the march 2010 budget)
- o £125,001 to £250,000 1%
- o £250,001 to £500,000 3%

o   £500,001 to £1000,000 4%
o   Over £1,000,000 from April 2011 5%

In certain areas, known as disadvantaged areas, which are defined by post code, information of which can be gained from the Revenue and Customs, there is no stamp duty payable on properties under £150,000. This is because of the need to regenerate these areas and thus encourage development.

Other costs

A solicitor normally carries out conveyancing of property. However, it is perfectly normal for individuals to do their own conveyancing. All the necessary paperwork can be obtained from legal stationers and it is executed on a step-by-step basis.

It has to be said that solicitors are now very competitive with their charges and, for the sake of between £250-£350 plus disbursements, it is better to let someone else do the work which allows you to concentrate on other things.

Land Registry

The Land Registry records all purchases of land in England and Wales and is open to the public (inspection of records, called a property search)

The registered title to any particular piece of land or property will carry with it a description and include the name of owner, mortgage, rights over other persons land and any other rights. There is a small charge for inspection.

A lot of solicitors have direct links and can carry out searches very quickly. Not all properties are registered although it is now a duty to register all transactions.

Searches

These are checks with the local authority and other bodies which ascertain whether or not there are any proposed developments or other works in the vicinity of the property which could jeopardise the value of the property in the future or the well being of the occupants.

There is normally a pro forma used for this as the questions are standard, and a charge of between £80-150 will be incurred.

Home information packs

Home Information packs, which have been phased in over a period of several months, are now compulsory (after 14th December 2007) for all properties being sold. Whoever is marketing the property, usually an estate agent, must have a HIP and provide prospective purchasers with a copy on request. It is estimated that the total costs of producing a Home Information pack will be between £300-£500.

At present, estate agents, and anyone else, is able to market properties once a HIP has been commissioned. After 31st may 2008, the estate agent, or person(s) selling the property will need to obtain an Energy Performance Certificate, title and plan and index before marketing the property.

Penalties and enforcement

The pack duties will be enforced by local authority Trading Standards Officers. They will be able to give advice and warnings, as well as issuing penalty notices. The fixed penalty has been set at £200 initially, and can be repeated if a breach is repeated. Marketing a property without a Home Information Pack, or an incomplete pack, will render an estate agent, or person(s) selling the property liable.

Estate agents should also be aware that a breach of the pack duties will be treated as 'undesirable practice' under the Estate Agents Act and must be notified to the Office of Fair Trading. An estate agent who consistently flouts the Pack duties will be likely to risk a banning order from the OFT.

How is a HIP obtained?

Professional sources include estate agents, solicitors, financial advisors and also specialist providers. You can also compile a HIP yourself.

You should see the official website, which contains exhaustive information about HIP's-www.homeinformationpacks.gov.uk. Large supermarkets who have entered the estate agency business such as Asda and Tesco plan to provide free packs as an inducement for people to use their services.

How do HIP's affect buyers?

In theory, having access to a Home Information pack will save time and money. Information that either you or your solicitor would need to obtain will be readily available. Buyers will not have to wait weeks for searches, such as council searches. In some cases, the seller may commission a structural survey, which again will save time and money, as long as the purchaser is happy to rely on the information.

The Home Information Pack-what it costs and what goes in it

COMPULSORY DOCUMENTS	WHAT IS IT?	WHERE DO YOU GET IT FROM?	COST
Home Information pack Index	Checklist of items in HIP	Do-It-Yourself	Nominal
Energy Performance Certificate	Property's rating for energy efficiency and environmental impact	Audit carried out by a professional energy assessor	£120-£130
Sale statement	Basic property information including address, the seller and whether it is freehold	Do-It-Yourself	Nominal
Local authority searches	Dossier of planning applications and local plans plus details of water provision	Planning information can be requested from local authority. Drainage and water searches obtained from water supplier. Contaminated land search also needed. Local authority can advise	£120-£140.
Evidence of title	Proof that seller owns the property	Land Registry	£10 Ls/d £20 Freehold
For leasehold sales	Copy of lease, service charge and lessor details	Lease from Land Registry other items from managing agent.	£125
Freehold total			**£250-£280**

Leasehold total			£420
OPTIONAL ITEMS			
Home condition report	Details about the property's physical condition	Qualified home inspector	£200 (typical three bed house)
Legal summary	Summary of legal documents in pack	Solicitor or conveyancer	£15-50
Home use/contents forms	Information on boundaries, services, sharing with neighbours, planning permissions and other matters of potential interest to buyers.	Forms from: www.homeinformationpacks.gov.uk or a solicitor or conveyancer.	Nominal
Other documents	For example, warranties and extra searches	Solicitor, conveyancer or personal search company.	Depends on searches required
Freehold overall total			**£465-£530**
Leasehold			**£605-£670**

Since the packs were first introduced, and then phased in to apply to all properties from 14th December 2007, there has been a barrage of criticism from many parties concerning their usefulness, with many seeing it as just an extra cost. However, given that a property is a very expensive purchase, and that problems after the purchase can be very distressing and costly, the basic principle of obtaining as much information as possible concerning the nature of the property, is a sound one. Obviously, as a home condition report is optional, it is very important to ensure that a report is obtained, either from the owner or from an independent source.

Energy Performance Certificates (EPC's)

EPC's are a compulsory part of a Home Information Pack. However, although they are part of a HIP, they have been compulsory for all rental homes since 1st October 2008. Therefore all landlords are required, after this date, to commission an EPC.

As seen above, an EPC surveyor will assess the property and looks at all the ways a house or flat can waste heat, such as inadequate loft insulation, lack of cavity wall insulation, draughts and obsolete boilers. After the assessment they will award a rating from A (as good as it gets) to G (terrible). The document also includes information and advice on how to improve matters, such as lagging the water tank or installing double-glazing. An EPC costs between £120-130 and is be valid for ten years. Improvements made while the certificate is in force will not need a new survey.

Structural surveys

The basic structural survey is the homebuyers survey and valuation which is normally carried out by the building society or other lender.

This will cost you between £300-400 and is not really an in-depth survey, merely allowing the lender to see whether they should lend or not, and how much they should lend. Sometimes, lenders keep what they refer to as a retention, which means that they will not forward the full value (less deposit) until certain defined works have been carried out.

If you want to go further than a homebuyers report then you will have to instruct a firm of surveyors who have several survey types, depending on how far you want to go and how much you want to spend.

A word of caution. Many people go rushing headlong into buying a flat or house. They are usually exhilarated and wish to complete their purchase fairly quickly in order to establish their new home. If you stop and think about this, it is complete folly and can prove very expensive later. A house or flat is a commodity, like other commodities, except that it is usually a lot more expensive. A lot can be wrong with the commodity that you have purchased which is not immediately obvious.

Only after you have completed the deal and paid over the odds for your purchase do you begin to regret what you have done.

The true price of a property is not what the estate agent is asking, certainly not what the seller is asking. The true market price is the difference between what a property similar to the one in good condition is being sold at and your property minus cost of works to bring it up to that value.

Therefore, if you have any doubts whatsoever, and if you can afford it, get a detailed survey of the property you are proposing to buy and get the works required costed out. When negotiating, this survey is an essential tool in order to arrive at an accurate and fair price. Do not rest faith in others, particularly when you alone stand to lose.

One further word of caution. As stated, a lot of problems with property cannot be seen. A structural survey will highlight those. In some cases it may not be wise to proceed at all.

Mortgage fees

Mortgage indemnity insurance. This is a one-off payment if you are arranging a mortgage over 70-80% of lenders valuation. This represents insurance taken out by the lender in case the purchaser defaults on payments, in which case the lender will sell the property to reclaim the loan. It is to protect the mortgage lender not the buyer.

The cost of the insurance varies depending on how much you borrow. A 90% mortgage on a £150,000 property will cost between £300-600. Always think about the relative economics. A lot of money is made by a lot of people in house buying and selling. The loser is usually the buyer or seller, not the host of middlemen. So think carefully about what you are doing.

Mortgage arrangement fees

Depending upon the type of mortgage you are considering you may have to pay an arrangement fee. You should budget for up to £500.

Removals

Unless you are not moving far and are considering doing it yourself, budget for hiring a removal firm. This will depend on how many possessions you have and how much time and money you have. Take care when choosing the removal firm. Choose one who comes recommended if possible.

There are other costs too. Reconnection of telephone lines and possibly a deposit, carpets, curtains and plumbing-in washing machines. How much you pay will probably depend on how handy you are yourself. There are also smaller incidental costs such as redirecting mail by the post office.

15

THE ROLE OF ESTATE AGENTS IN BUYING AND SELLING PROPERTY

Estate Agents

What to expect from an estate agent:

- Advice on the selling or asking price of a house or flat - they know the local market
- Advice on the best way to sell (or buy) and where to advertise; they should discuss an advertising budget with you
- If selling, a meeting to visit, assess and value your home and also to take down the particulars of your home. The Property Misdescriptions Act, which arose out of the bad old days of the 1980's, prevents agents from using ambiguous statements to enhance the sale of the property. You should look at the points carefully as people who are disappointed after reading such a glowing report will not purchase.
- They may ask for details of recent bills, such as council tax and electricity. They should also be willing to give advice on fixtures and fittings included in the sale.
- They should be willing to show potential buyers around your home if you are not available.
- Don't expect to have to pay for a for-sale board although some lenders will try to make a charge.

Choosing an agent if selling

Consider the following points:

- They ought to sell your type of property or specialise in one particular area of the market
- They should be a member of one of the professional bodies such as the National Association of Estate Agents, the Royal Institution of

Chartered Surveyors, The Incorporated Society of Valuers and Auctioneers, The Architects and Surveyors Institute or the Association of Building Engineers.

- Obtain quotes of fees, including the basic charge and any extras you might have to pay for, such as advertising in specialist publications.

- Choose at least two agents to value the house, if instructing an agent.

Selling through one or more agents
Sole agency.
Offering an agent sole agency may reduce the fee. This can be done for a limited time. After this you can instruct multiple agents. With sole agency you can sell privately.

Joint sole agents
With this arrangement, two or more agents co-operate in the house sale and split the commission. The agents may charge a higher commission in this case.

Multiple agency
This means that you have several agents trying to sell your home, but only pay the agent who sells your property.

Buying property using the internet
There are a number of websites that also detail properties, some are independent and some are owned by the large players. The following are a selection of the main sites:

www.rightmove.co.uk.
This is one of the largest sites, jointly owned and run by Halifax, Royal Sun Alliance, Connell and Countryside assured Group.

www.assertahome.co.uk
This is owned by the Commercial Union and Norwich Union Insurance Groups. The claims of the website are that it can help the buyer to find a

property, move home and settle in. There are links to the Insurance Broker, John Charcoal.

www.propertyfinder.co.uk
This site began life in 1995 and is connected to several prominent estate agency groups.

www.primelocation.co.uk
This site was launched in 2000 by a consortium of estate agents. This site deals with more expensive properties.

Selling property using the internet

Although estate agents are still the main avenues for selling property, as we have seen, the web is beginning to play a more significant part. In addition to the websites detailed, almost all agents now have their own website. This is really an electronic shop window where your property is displayed. Buyers interested in your property should be able to e-mail the estate agent directly for a viewing.

16

MORTGAGES

Most people purchasing a property will need a mortgage. There are fewer products on the markets in 2010. However, it is crucial that you are in possession of all the facts when making a decision about a mortgage.

Financial advisers will give you plenty of advice but not always the best advice. Sometimes it is better to go to the lender direct. Before you talk to lenders, work out what your priorities are, such as tax advantage, investment potential, early repayment and so on. Make sure that you are aware of the costs of life cover.

Lenders-Banks and building societies
There is little or no difference between the mortgages offered by banks and building societies.

Because banks borrow against the wholesale money markets, the interest rate they charge to borrowers will fluctuate (unless fixed) as and when their base rate changes. Building societies however, which will rely more heavily on their savers deposits to fund their lending, may adjust the interest rate charged for variable mortgages only once a year. This may be a benefit or disadvantage, depending on whether rates are going up or down.

Centralised lenders
Centralised lenders borrow from the money markets to fund their lending and have no need for the branch network operated by banks and building societies. Centralised lenders, who came to the fore during the 1980s, particularly the house price boom, have been criticised for being quick to implement increases but slow to implement decreases, through rate reductions. This is, simply, because they exist to make profit. Therefore, you should be cautious indeed before embarking on a mortgage with lenders of this kind.

Brokers and "independent" financial advisors

Brokers act as intermediaries between potential borrowers and mortgage providers. If they are "tied" agents they can only advise on the products of one bank, insurance company or building society. If they are independent they should, technically, advise and recommend on every product in the market place.

A word of warning. It is up to you to ask detailed questions about any product a broker offers you. You should ask if they will receive a fee or commission, or both for any sale they arrange for you. Many brokers sell unsuitable products because they receive healthy commissions.

How much can you borrow

There is a standard calculation for working out the maximum mortgage that you will be allowed. Three times annual salary, for a joint mortgage, or two or two and a half times combined used to be the norm, and in 2010 banks have reverted to this following the sub-prime fiasco.

The lender will typically charge between £100-300 for setting up the mortgage. In many cases, charges can be added to the amount borrowed.

Deposits

Banks and building societies are lending less nowadays and require higher deposits. Lenders dealing with buy-to-let mortgages will usually ask for a minimum of 15% deposit. The more that you put down the better deal that you are likely to get from the lender.

When exchanging contracts on a property it is usual to pay 10% of the sale price to the seller's solicitor.

Joint mortgages

If you want a joint mortgage, as for any other shared loan you and your partner have a shared responsibility for ensuring that the necessary repayments are made. If something happens to one partner then the other has total responsibility for the loan.

Standard payment options

There are three main methods of determining interest rates for mortgages:

- Variable rate: the interest rate of the borrowed capital follows the changes in a variable rate set by the lender. This can change at any time. The rate that you are charged is set a t a level either above or below the Standard variable rate (SVR)

- Tracker rate: the interest follows an external tracker, such as the bank of England base rate (LIBOR). Any change made to those rates is applied instantly to your own mortgage rate.
- Fixed rate: your interest rate remains at a fixed amount, and does not change.

There are additional options which can be applied in conjunction with the above:

- Capped rate mortgages where the rate has a limit, either higher or lower beyond which it cannot pass.
- Discount rate where the rate is set lower for a certain initial term of the mortgage.
- Offset mortgage which takes into account savings when determining interest rates on a mortgage. Any savings held are deducted from mortgage borrowings reducing the rate of interest on your mortgage.
- Current Account Mortgages (CAM). A CAM is similar to an offset mortgage, but in this case the current account and mortgage are merged together. Income is usually required to pay into this type of account, with any savings in the account deducted from the total of the mortgage.

Endowment mortgages
With this, now largely discredited, type of mortgage, you have to take out an endowment insurance policy which is then used to pay off the mortgage loan in a lump sum at the end of the term. There are a number of different types designed to achieve the same end:

- Low cost with profits. This is the usual sort of endowment, guaranteeing to pay back part of the loan only. However, because bonuses are likely to be added, it is usually enough to pay off the loan in full;

- Unit linked endowment. With this, the monthly premiums are used to buy units in investment funds. The drawback is that there is no guarantee how much the policy will be worth on maturity, since this depends on how well the investments have performed.

A word of warning. Endowment products were pushed heavily by financial brokers. There was an obsession with them in the 1980's. This is because they earn big commission for those people that sell them. Like all good salespeople, advisers failed to reveal the down sides.

These are:

Endowments are investment linked and there is no guarantee that they will have matured sufficiently at the end of the term to repay the mortgage. This leaves you in a mess. A repayment mortgage will definitely have paid off the mortgage at the end of the term.

If you change your mortgage and decide that you do not wish to continue with an endowment mortgage, and so cash in the policy early you will almost certainly get a poor return unless it is close to maturity. In the early years of the policy, most of your payments will go towards administration and commission (a fact that your broker does not always reveal) The alternative in these circumstances is to maintain the endowment until it matures, treating it as a stand alone investment which will, hopefully, make you some money eventually.

Repayment mortgages
This mortgage, where the borrower makes regular repayments to pay the mortgage off over the term is a fairly safe bet. However, if you plan to move house every five years then this will not necessarily be the best mortgage for you. With a repayment mortgage, you pay interest every month but only a small proportion of the capital, particularly in the early years of the mortgage.

Pension mortgages
Similar to the other products except that the payments go into a personal pension plan with the remainder after paying the mortgage forming the basis of a pension. The same characteristics apply as to the others.

Interest only mortgage
The borrower pays interest only on the loan, and decides how he or she will pay the loan off at the end. The lender will want to know this too.

These types of mortgage are becoming more popular, again as a result of the high cost of housing and increased repayments.

Foreign currency mortgages

Some foreign banks offer short-term mortgages in the foreign currency of that bank. Their lending criteria can be much more relaxed than trying to borrow from a British lender. The advantage of this sort of mortgage depends on currency fluctuations. If the pound is stable or rises, the borrower benefits. If the pound drops, the borrower will have to pay more.

These types of home loans should be left to more sophisticated investors as there is the potential to get into trouble unless you have a clear grasp on the implications of such a mortgage.

Cashbacks

You have probably seen the adverts offering large sums of cashback if you take a particular product. If you read the small print, unless you take the highest mortgage available with the highest deposit then you will not get anywhere near such a sum.

You should remember that money given with one hand is money taken back with another. If you decide to take up such a mortgage, then see what you will get back and see what the terms are, i.e., interest rates and so on.

What to do if you feel that you have been given wrong advice

The mortgage lending market is very complicated and many people have suffered at the hands of financial advisors and others who have given incorrect advice. Mortgage regulation has not been very tight. However, the basic framework is as follows:

- Sales of mortgage linked investments like endowments or pensions are regulated by the Financial Services Authority. Anyone selling investments must be qualified and registered and must be able to clearly demonstrate that the policy that they have recommended is suitable. All registered individuals and firms are inspected by regulators and can be fined or expelled from the industry if guilty of wrongly selling products.

- By contrast, information on mortgages is currently regulated by the industry only, voluntarily, under a code of mortgage practice sponsored by the Council of Mortgage Lenders. Although most of the big players are signed up to the code there are still some who are not. Check first before taking advice.

17

THE LAW AND OWNER OCCUPIERS COMMONHOLD, FREEHOLD AND LEASEHOLD

Commonhold and Leasehold Reform Act 2002

The Commonhold and Leasehold Reform Act 2002 introduced into English law an entirely new form of tenure, namely commonhold. It is specifically targeted at blocks of flats, where leasehold has been the normal form of tenure until now.

The Government hopes that commonhold will avoid the tensions and conflicts that have sometimes arisen between leaseholders and freeholders. Time will tell whether that hope will be realised. If it is, doubtless commonhold will come to supersede leasehold as the normal form of tenure for premises divided into flats. For the present, however, commonhold and leasehold regimes will operate side by side, with leasehold predominating.

But it would be very reasonable for a flat owner to say at this point, "Wait a minute. Commonhold has been brought in as an alternative to leasehold; but what was wrong with leasehold? And why do I have to trouble myself with all this anyway? Why can't I simply own my flat, the same way as other people own their houses?"

This is a very fair question. To answer it, we need to look at how the law regards property ownership.

Freehold and Leasehold

The law does not look at property in the same way as most lay people. Most people think in terms of houses and other buildings; the law is more interested in the land beneath. A freehold home owner will say "I own my house." But the law will say "He owns the land on which is built the house he lives in." To the law, the key point is that he owns the land - the buildings on it are incidental.

For practical purposes, the strongest form of title to land is that of freehold. Freehold title lasts forever; it may be bought and sold, or passed by inheritance. In short, freehold title is tantamount to outright ownership, and is taken as such for the purposes of this book.

Freeholders may, of course, use their land for their own purposes. The freehold home owner is merely the most familiar example. But they may also, if they wish, allow other people to use their land. And this is where leases, and other forms of tenure, come in.

Suppose you would like to make use of a piece of land owned by someone else. The owner is unwilling to sell it to you, but, having no immediate use for it himself, is willing to allow you to use it for a time, perhaps in exchange for payment. At its simplest, this arrangement implies no more than a licence - the owner's (i.e. landlord's) permission for you to be on his land.

But such a licence can be revoked by the landlord at any time, with or without a good reason. As such it is not very valuable, so if the owner wants to make money by allowing other people to use his land, he needs to give them a legal status that they will be willing to pay for. This is achieved by granting a lease or tenancy. It should be noted here that, from the legal point of view, a lease and a tenancy are the same thing; but in practice, the terms tend to be used in different contexts. This is explained below: for the present, we shall call it a lease.

A lease grants the leaseholder permission to use the land for a certain period, which can be anything from a day or two to several thousand years. It will usually attach conditions, for example that the leaseholder must pay rent (usually a sum of money, although in principle other goods or services could constitute rent).

The lease may, but does not have to, put certain restrictions on what the leaseholder may do with the land. But it must, in order to be a lease rather than merely a licence, grant the leaseholder 'exclusive possession'. This is the right to exclude other people, especially the landlord, from the land. Such a right need not be absolute, and exceptions to it are explained later in the book: but it is enough to give the leaseholder a high degree of control over the land, which has become, for the duration of the lease, very much the leaseholder's land rather than the freeholder's. A lease, unless it contains a stipulation to the contrary, may be bought, sold, or inherited; if this happens, all the rights and duties under it pass to the new owner.

Leases and Tenancies

Confusion is often caused by the fact that, although the terms leaseholder (or lessee) and tenant are legally interchangeable, they tend to be used in different senses. The tendency is to refer to short leases as tenancies: the more substantial the rights conferred, and the longer the period for which they run, the likelier it is that the agreement will be referred to as a lease. For the purposes of this book, an agreement will be referred to as a 'tenancy' if it is periodic or runs for a fixed term of less than seven years. A fixed term agreement running for more than seven years will be referred to as a 'lease'.

A 'periodic' tenancy is one that runs from period to period (usually, from week to week or month to month) until something intervenes to stop it, and is conditional on payment of rent. A tenancy that runs for a fixed term of less than seven years has a definite date of expiry but is otherwise similar to a periodic tenancy and will depend on regular payment of rent. Tenancies granted by local authorities and housing associations tend to be periodic; private landlords generally grant either periodic tenancies or short fixed-term tenancies (typically, six months). At any rate, the landlord of a periodic or short-term tenancy will usually accept most of the responsibility for maintaining the property and will charge a relatively high rent to allow for this. If the tenancy is for residential property, the landlord's duty to maintain the dwelling is imposed by law (Landlord and Tenant Act 1985).

It is common for private landlords to insist on prepayment of rent or a deposit before granting a tenancy, and many landlords will levy a separate service charge to cover the cost of some activities that are peripheral to the central one of providing housing; but despite these costs it would be true to say that the principal financial responsibility accepted by a periodic or short-term tenant is that of paying the rent.

The position of a leaseholder is very different. The major financial commitment will usually be a substantial initial payment either to the landlord (if the lease is newly created) or to the previous leaseholder. There is still a rent, called a ground rent, payable to the landlord, but it is usually a notional amount (£50 or £100 a year is not uncommon). Its purpose is not so much to give the landlord an income as to give the leaseholder an annual reminder that ultimate ownership of the land is not his.

Types of Leasehold Property

In the context of residential property, it should be noted that the great majority of leases relate to flats rather than houses. This is because of the legal concept of land tenure as described above. If a builder buys some freehold land and covers it in houses, it is possible to parcel out the area so that each bit of freehold land, and the house standing on it, can be sold separately. It does not matter if the houses are semi-detached or terraced, because there is well-established law governing party walls of adjoining freeholders. But if there are flats, the builder has a problem: how can the flats be sold since they cannot be said to stand on separate and distinct bits of land? The answer is to sell leases.

Where flats are sold, each purchaser acquires a lease that gives him specified rights over the parcel of land on which the flats stand. These rights, of course, are shared by the leaseholders of the other flats. In addition, however, each leaseholder gains the right to exclusive possession of part of the building occupying the land - his own flat. The leaseholder would say "I own my flat", but the law says "He owns a lease granting him certain rights, in particular that of access, to a defined parcel of land and the right of exclusive possession of specified parts of a building erected on that land." This may seem a slightly unusual way of looking at it, but it is fundamental to understanding the way that the law sees the relationship between leaseholders of flats and their freeholders.

The freehold of flatted property will often be retained by the developer, although sometimes it will be sold to a property company. Formerly, it was common practice for the freehold to be retained even when separate houses were built. This allowed the freeholder to retain an interest in the property and, above all, to regain full possession of it when the lease expired. However, the position of freeholders has been weakened by three key pieces of legislation, the Leasehold Reform Act 1967, the Leasehold Reform, Housing and Urban Development Act 1993, and the Commonhold and Leasehold Reform Act 2002. These Acts are described in detail further on: their overall effect is to entitle leaseholders either to the freehold of houses or to a new lease of flats. In view of the legislation, there is now little point in the original owner's attempting to retain the freehold of land on which houses have been built. The exception is where a house is sold on the basis of shared ownership - see below.

Most residential leasehold property therefore consists of flats. Of these, most are in the private sector, comprising purpose-built blocks and (especially in London) conversions of what were once large single houses. The freehold will usually belong to the developer, to a property company, or sometimes to the original owner of the site.

House leases normally give most of the repairing responsibility to the leaseholder - services provided by the freeholder, and therefore service charges, are minimal. In flats, however, although the leaseholder will normally be responsible for the interior of the flat, the freeholder will maintain the fabric of the building and will recoup the costs of doing so by levying service charges on the leaseholders. This is an area of such potential conflict between leaseholders and freeholders that it has been the subject of legislation. It is dealt with fully further on in the book.

Mixed-tenure blocks: the right to buy

The general shift from renting to owning means that sometimes flats have been sold in blocks that were originally developed for letting to tenants: the result is often a 'mixed-tenure' block, with both leaseholders and tenants. Although this sometimes happens in the private sector, it is particularly common in blocks owned by local authorities and housing associations, for it is to these that the statutory right to buy applies. This right was created by the Housing Act 1980 and allows most local authority tenants, and some housing association tenants, to buy their homes at a heavily discounted price. Tenants of houses are normally sold the freehold, but tenants of flats become leaseholders.

Shared ownership

Another result of the trend towards home ownership has been the dramatic expansion of shared ownership. This is a form of tenure that combines leasing and renting. However, the term 'shared ownership' is something of a misnomer because ownership is not, in fact, shared between the leaseholder and the freeholder. The lease relates to the whole property, not part of it, and the shared owner is as entitled as any other leaseholder to consider himself the owner of his house. The key point about shared ownership leases is not that they give an inferior form of tenure to other leases but that they have different conditions attached. The leaseholder pays less than the full value of the lease; typically, half. In exchange for this concession, he pays not the normal notional ground rent but a much more substantial rent. However, he is much more a leaseholder than he is a tenant, and, like other leaseholders (but unlike tenants) is responsible for the internal repair of the property and, in the case of houses, usually the fabric of the building too.

Shared owners usually have the right to increase their stake as and when they can afford it: this is called 'staircasing' because the owner's share goes up in steps. If the property is a house, the freehold will normally be transferred when the owner's share reaches 100%, and he will then be in the same position as any other freehold home owner. If it is a flat, he will continue to be a leaseholder but there will no longer be a rental (other than ground rent).

Head Leases and Subleases

For the sake of clarity and brevity, this book has been written throughout on the basis that there are only two parties involved: the freeholder and the leaseholder. Usually this picture is accurate; but it is the right of the leaseholder, unless the lease specifically forbids it, to sublet the property, or part of it, to someone else. This means that the leaseholder delegates some of his rights over the property to another person. Obviously, he cannot delegate rights greater than his own, so that if he holds a lease of the property running until 2025 he cannot grant a sublease running until 2050. And he cannot grant a sublease of the whole of his rights because this would leave him with no interest in the property: it would, in fact, amount to the same as an assignment. So it is necessary for a sublease that the original leaseholder be left with something; either some period of time or some part of the property.

It is possible in theory to have a whole hierarchy of leases applying to a particular property, starting with the freehold, then the head lease, then a sublease, followed by sub-subleases and possibly sub-sub-subleases below those. There are two rules that limit this kind of proliferation: one, explained above, is that each lease must confer less, in space or time or both, than the one above it; and the other, that is a lease may not be held by the same person as holds the lease (or freehold) immediately above it.

Commonhold

To try to deal with problems arising from the relationship between freeholders and leaseholders, a new form of tenure, 'commonhold', was created by the Commonhold and Leasehold Reform Act 2002. It is designed specifically for use in blocks of flats, and the idea is that all the individual flat owners (or 'unit holders', as the Act calls them) will belong to a 'commonhold association', a registered company that operate under a constitution (the 'memorandum and articles') and act in accordance with a 'commonhold community statement'. This arrangement ensures that each unit holder will have two separate interests in relation to the property: individually, in his own particular unit, and collectively, in the block as a whole. The relevant parts of the 2002 Act will not be implemented until October 2003 at the earliest, and even after that it will take some time for new commonhold developments to start operating, so it will be some years before commonhold will really be put to the test. Meanwhile, the Government is consulting about detailed regulations for commonhold, including the standard constitution (memorandum and articles) for commonhold associations, and the standard form for commonhold community statements. At the time of writing it seems likely that these standard documents will be very detailed and specific.

The standard forms include some welcome recognition that disputes will inevitably occur within commonhold schemes, and disputes will be referred to an ombudsman, but it still seems likely that the commonhold association will be struggling to find an effective remedy when individual unit holders default on their obligations. This remains a major concern about the future effectiveness of the commonhold system.

It is be possible to register newly developed blocks as commonhold, but it will be virtually impossible to convert existing blocks to commonhold because the 2002 Act requires unanimous consent, something that is unlikely to be achieved. Therefore, unless the rules are changed again it seems that leasehold will remain the dominant form of tenure for flats for many years to come. However, reasons are given in the last Chapter for believing that commonhold is unlikely to result in the benefits its promoters have claimed for it.

18

OBLIGATIONS OF FREEHOLDER AND LEASEHOLDER

General Principles

For centuries the law did little to regulate the relationship between freeholders and leaseholders. The view was taken that they had entered into the relationship of their own free will, and it was up to them to agree whatever terms and conditions they liked. If either party did not keep the bargain, he could of course be sued in the courts, but, on the whole, the law did not interfere in the bargain itself.

In the twentieth century, however, the view grew up that some types of bargain are inherently unfair and even those that are not might still be open to exploitation.

An example of the first type is an agreement that residential property will revert to the original freeholder at the end of a long lease. This meant that when 99-year leases expired, leaseholders found that their homes had abruptly returned to the outright ownership of the heir of the original freeholder, leaving them as mere trespassers liable to be ejected at any time. In practice, freeholders were usually willing to grant a fresh lease, but sometimes only at a very high price that the leaseholder might well be unable to afford. In some cases, freeholders insisted on reclaiming the property however much the leaseholder offered, and the law supported them. This is the state of affairs that led to legislation entitling almost all residential leaseholders to extend their leases, and many of them to claim the freehold.

The freeholder's right to demand a service charge is an example of an arrangement that is fair in principle but open to abuse in practice. It is inevitable, especially in flats, that responsibility for some types of repair cannot be ascribed to any individual leaseholder and must therefore be retained by the freeholder; who must, in turn, recoup the cost from leaseholders. However, some freeholders abused this system by levying extravagant service charges that made the service charge a source of profit. To prevent this, there is now a substantial body of legislation designed to ensure that freeholders carry out only the works that are really necessary and that they recover their legitimate costs and no more. The complicated rules governing this are chiefly found in the Landlord and Tenant Act 1985 (as amended) and are described in Chapter Three.

Under the Landlord and Tenant Act 1987, either party to a long lease (one originally granted for at least 21 years) may go to the Leasehold Valuation Tribunal (or 'LVT') to argue that the lease is deficient in some way and needs to be changed. If only the one lease is affected, the tribunal may vary it. Sometimes, however, a number of leases may need to be changed; in this case either the freeholder or 75% of the leaseholders may apply.

Obligations of Leaseholders

The obligations of leaseholders are set out in the lease; indeed, since it is a document drafted by or on behalf of freeholders, one of its main aims is to tell leaseholders what they must and must not do. However, legislation and judicial decisions sometimes come to the leaseholder's assistance.

Consumer legislation can also apply to leases; in particular, the Unfair Terms in Consumer Contracts Regulations 1999 (which replace earlier regulations made in 1995) have a major impact. These apply to standard terms in contracts. This means they normally cover the terms of leases, which are usually presented to potential leaseholders as a package with no opportunity to renegotiate individual terms. Occasionally, however, individual terms can be specifically negotiated and it should be noted that in that case the Unfair Terms Regulations do not apply. Nor will they apply to any lease granted before the earlier version of the regulations which came in July 1995. The Office of Fair Trading has issued advice about the types of term that are likely to be judged unfair in the context of assured tenancies. The OFT has not issued advice about long leases, but it is likely that similar standards would apply.

a: Plain and intelligible language

Over many years property lawyers have developed an obscure and technical language that can have the effect of excluding outsiders. This form of 'legalese' is characterised by unwieldy sentences with few (or no) commas to break them up, long lists often consisting of different names for the same thing, and a vocabulary of unfamiliar words and (worst of all) familiar words given unfamiliar meanings.

For instance, in normal English the verb 'determine' means 'ascertain' or 'firmly decide', but when a property lawyer applies it to a lease it means 'end' or 'terminate' (as in 'the lease shall determine if...'). Property lawyers also have a well-merited reputation for using words like 'hereinafter' and 'aforesaid', which, although not ambiguous, are hardly everyday English, while occasional outbreaks of Latin are not unknown (*pari passu* and *mutatis mutandis*).

Thankfully, this style is going out of fashion and an increasing number of modern leases are being written in more intelligible language, and for leases made since 1995 the Unfair Terms Regulations mean that arcanely written terms may be unenforceable. However, a huge number of leases written in traditional style still have decades or even centuries to run, so unfortunately property lawyers' English will be with us for a long time yet.

b: Terms Unfair on Consumers

There are some terms to which the Office of Fair Trading objects in any consumer contract. These are terms that place an unreasonable burden on the customer (the leaseholder) or give an unfair advantage to the supplier (the freeholder). Some of these terms are common in long leases.

There may be a clause in which the leaseholder declares that he has 'read and understood' the lease, even though the document is long and complex and it unlikely that anyone would read (or understand) the whole of it. The aim is to put the leaseholder at a disadvantage in any dispute by arguing that he was fully aware of all the terms of the lease. Another way of loading the scales is a clause allowing the freeholder the final decision about vital matters, such as whether or not the freeholder and the leaseholder have fulfilled their respective obligations under the lease.

These clauses are probably unenforceable in leases made since July 1995, but in earlier leases they are probably valid.

There are other types of clause that are potentially a problem for the leaseholder. An example is a clause laying down procedural formalities. Such a clause is not necessarily a problem: for instance, leases commonly require formal communications between the freeholder and the leaseholder to be in writing, and this is a perfectly reasonable requirement because it reduces the chances misunderstandings or disputes about who said what. But it is harder to justify a requirement for notices to be sent by registered post, and some leases stipulate procedures that are so onerous that the aim seems to be to deter leaseholders from exercising their rights.

Similar comments apply to clauses imposing financial penalties for breaches of the lease. This is not necessarily unreasonable, but sometimes the penalties are out of all proportion to the nature of the breach.

Some leases require the leaseholder to join with the freeholder (and help with the cost) in responding to legal or other notices pertaining to the property. Again, this may be reasonable in some circumstances, but as a blanket requirement it can act against leaseholders' interests.

An interesting and debatable issue is the prohibition of set-off, which is a standard clause in most leases. 'Set-off' is the practice of deducting (or 'setting off') from any payment made by one party under an agreement any sums that are owed by the other party. For instance, suppose a leaseholder considers that a repair to the fabric of the building is the freeholder's responsibility, but the freeholder either disputes this or fails to take any action. Eventually the leaseholder does the work at his own expense, and next time the annual service charge falls due he reimburses himself by deducting, or 'setting off', the cost from his service charge payment.

Leaseholders like set-off because it is an easy way of reclaiming disputed sums from the freeholder, and it shifts onto the freeholder the onus of continuing the dispute. Freeholders dislike it for exactly the same reasons, which is why leases normally prohibit it. The Office of Fair Trading, in its advice on assured tenancies, says that prohibiting set-off is unfair, but it is not clear whether the same advice would apply to leases.

The possibility that unfair, or potentially unfair, clauses will feature in a lease underlines the need for competent legal advice before signing it. An experienced solicitor will be able to advise whether doubtful clauses can be, or are likely to be, used against leaseholders. Leaseholders may also have remedies available under the Landlord and Tenant Act: this is covered below and, in the key area of service charges, in the next Chapter.

c: Restrictive clauses in leases
So far, we have looked at leases as if they were consumer contracts, and outlined some of the clauses they may contain that could affect

leaseholders in their capacity as consumers. But there are some further potentially difficult terms that relate specifically to property issues. These terms are not necessarily unreasonable. For example, in a lease concerning an upstairs flat it would be quite normal to have a clause requiring the leaseholder to keep the premises carpeted. This makes sense because bare floors, although currently very fashionable, could be very noisy for the people in the flat below.

The Office of Fair Trading's advice identifies several types of sweeping provisions that would, if they were enforced, considerably restrict the tenant's ability to live a normal life. Although the OFT's advice relates to assured tenancies, similar objections would probably apply to these clauses in leases. For example:

- **Pets** Leases often lay down that the leaseholder may not own pets, or may not do so without the freeholder's permission.

- **Upkeep** Leases may say that the leaseholder must decorate periodically - say, every five or seven years. Where there is a garden, it is common for the leaseholder to be required to keep it in good order.

- **Business** Leases often lay down that the leaseholder must not run any sort of business from his home.

- **Use as residence** A lease will generally say that the property is to be used for the residential purposes of the leaseholder and his household, and that it cannot be sublet. It will sometimes attempt to restrict how many people may live there apart from the leaseholder.

- **Other** Leases sometimes forbid such things as the keeping of flammable materials and the installation of television aerials or satellite dishes. They may require leaseholders to drain hot water systems whenever they are away, or keep the premises clean and free of dust.

It is easy to see why freeholders want such clauses in the lease: it is because they realise that there will be serious problems if someone attempts, for instance, to keep four alsatians in a studio flat. The neighbours will be inconvenienced and will complain to the freeholder, and leases of other flats in the same block will become difficult to sell.

The same arguments could apply if one of the leaseholders allows his flat to fall into complete decorative decay or if he runs a noisy and busy trade from his home.

But the kind of blanket rules that appear in many leases go too far. A rule against any pets at all forbids not only four noisy alsatians but also entirely inoffensive pets such as a budgie or a goldfish. In the same way, prohibiting business activities means that the leaseholder may not use his home to write a book for publication, or address envelopes, and so on - types of home working that could not possibly inconvenience anyone.

The rule against sub-letting also prevents leaseholders from exploiting the value of their property by letting it out, something that is open to most home-owners and is increasingly accepted as normal.

For leases made since July 1995, these sweeping clauses are probably unfair and unenforceable. But even for older leases, the reality is that such broad provisions are seldom enforced. Freeholders, and their lawyers, like them because they feel that they preserve their freedom of action, allowing them to decide whether or not to enforce the lease if it is clear that one of these blanket conditions is being broken. But there are two problems with this attitude.

The first is that it creates uncertainty in the minds of leaseholders. Suppose the leases in a block of flats prohibit all pets, but leaseholder A has a goldfish and no action has been taken even though the freeholder is aware of the infringement. Leaseholder B may well conclude that there will be no objection if he gets a cat. If still there is no action, leaseholder C may feel able to get a couple of dogs - and so on. So the fact that restrictions are so broad can have the paradoxical effect of reducing their effectiveness.

The second problem is that if, in the example just given, the freeholder takes legal action to force C to get rid of the dogs, it is possible that C will argue in court that the treatment of the other leaseholders shows that the freeholder is not seriously interested in banning pets and that the action has been motivated rather by petty spite or bias.

It would be better if freeholders and their lawyers drafted leases that say what they mean: not that leaseholders may have no pets at all, but that they may have no pets apt to damage the property or cause inconvenience or annoyance to other persons. The same principle should apply to clauses dealing with sub-letting or working from home.

It is unfortunate that this book is forced to advise leaseholders to ignore some parts of their leases. The responsibility for this, however, lies with freeholders and their lawyers for writing into standard leases blanket conditions purporting to prohibit entirely inoffensive behaviour. This practice makes it inevitable, in the real world that leaseholders will disregard certain clauses, and that books like this will have to give them some indication of when they can probably do so safely. Most leaseholders exercise common sense and realise that the freeholder is unlikely to take action unless there is a complaint, which means that the leaseholder may do almost whatever he pleases provided he refrains from provoking anyone. It is sensible to stay on good terms with neighbours to ensure that if anything is bothering them they take it up directly with you rather than report the matter to the freeholder. Other leaseholders will also be able to tell you what view has been taken in the past - both by other residents and by the freeholder - in doubtful cases.

d: Restrictions on sale

Some leases restrict the kind of person to whom the lease may be sold (or 'assigned' - see below). For example, a housing scheme may have been intended specifically for the elderly. Clearly, it will not be maintained as such if leaseholders are free to assign or bequeath their leases to whomever they please, so the lease will say that it may be assigned only to persons above a certain age, and that if it is inherited by anyone outside the age group it must be sold on to someone qualified to hold it. Although this could be described as an onerous term because it makes it more difficult to find a buyer and may reduce the lease's value, it is reasonable given the need to ensure that the scheme continues to house elderly people exclusively. And the restriction it imposes is not too severe because so many potential purchasers qualify.

However, some leases define much more narrowly to whom they may be sold. Sometimes the freeholder is a body owned and run by the leaseholders themselves, and in these cases it is usual to require that all leaseholders must join the organisation and, if they leave it, must immediately dispose of the lease to someone that is willing to join. Again, such a term is not necessarily unacceptable. If the organisation makes relatively light demands on its members (perhaps no more than a modest admission fee or annual subscription), the restriction is unlikely greatly to diminish the value of the lease. If, however, the organisation expects much more from its members - perhaps that they actively take part in running it, or that they pay a large annual subscription - the value of the lease will be severely reduced because it will be difficult to find purchasers willing to accept the conditions. A key point is whether the organisation has power to expel members, thus forcing them to sell; and, if so, in what circumstances and by whom this power can be exercised.

e: Access

Virtually any lease will contain a clause allowing the freeholder to enter the property in order to inspect or repair it. This has the effect of qualifying the leaseholder's right of exclusive possession (see below), but only subject to certain conditions. The freeholder (or the freeholder's servants, such as agents or contractors) may enter only at reasonable times, and subject to the giving of reasonable notice. If these conditions are not met, the leaseholder is under no obligation to allow them in; and, even when the conditions are met, the landlord will be trespassing if he enters the property without the leaseholder's consent. If the leaseholder refuses consent even though the time is reasonable and reasonable notice has been given, the landlord's remedy is to get a court order against the leaseholder compelling him to grant entry. It is probable, in such a case, that the landlord will seek, and get, an award of legal costs against the leaseholder.

f: Arbitration

Many leases contain clauses providing that disputes can be submitted to arbitration at the request of either party. By the Commonhold and Leasehold Reform Act, the effect of these clauses is limited, because the results will not be binding so far as the Leasehold Valuation Tribunal is concerned. If, however, once a dispute has arisen, the parties to agree to submit it to an agreed arbitrator, they are bound by the result, which is enforceable by the courts. If such a 'post-dispute' arbitration finds that the leaseholder is in breach, this is equivalent to a finding by the LVT and will (if the other requirements are met) allow the freeholder to proceed with forfeiture. Arbitration may be a useful mechanism in some cases, and it may be cheaper and quicker than legal action, but it may be difficult to find an arbitrator in whom both parties have confidence.

Obligations of Freeholders

a: Exclusive possession and quiet enjoyment

The first and most important obligation on the freeholder, without which there would be no legal lease at all, is to respect the leaseholder's rights of 'exclusive possession' and 'quiet enjoyment'. Exclusive possession is the right to occupy the property and exclude others from it, especially the freeholder. Quiet enjoyment is another way of underlining the leaseholder's rights over the property: it means that the freeholder may not interfere with the leaseholder's use of the property provided that the terms of the lease are observed.

However, the leaseholder's right to quiet enjoyment applies only to breaches by the freeholder or the freeholder's servants such as agents or contractors. It is important to note this because the term is sometimes thought to mean that the freeholder must protect the leaseholder against any activity by anyone that interferes with his use of the property: this is not so. For example, if the freeholder carries out some activity elsewhere in the building that interferes with the leaseholder, the leaseholder's right to quiet enjoyment has been breached and he is entitled to redress unless the freeholder can show that the activity was necessary, for instance to comply with repairing obligations under the lease. But if the interference is caused by someone else, perhaps another leaseholder, the freeholder's obligation to provide quiet enjoyment has not been breached. And it is worth stressing in this connection that even if the other leaseholder is in breach of his lease, it is entirely up to the freeholder whether or not to take action: other leaseholders have no power to force the freeholder to deal with the situation.

This means that if one leaseholder is breaking his lease by holding noisy parties late at night, the other leaseholders may ask, but may not require, the freeholder to take action to enforce the lease. They may, however, take legal action directly against the offending leaseholder for nuisance.

b: The 'section 48' notice

Another important protection for leaseholders is found in section 48 of the Landlord and Tenant Act 1987. This was designed to deal with the situation in which freeholders seek to avoid their responsibilities by (to put it bluntly) doing a disappearing act. Sometimes freeholders would provide no address or telephone number or other means of contact, meaning that leaseholders were unable to hold the freeholder to his side of the agreement. Sections 47 and 48 therefore lay down that the freeholder must formally notify the leaseholder of his name and give an address within England and Wales at which he can be contacted, and that this information must be repeated on every demand for rent or service charge. This has proved especially valuable for leaseholders where the freeholder lives abroad, or is a company based abroad. It should be noted that the address does not have to be the freeholder's home, nor, if the freeholder is a company, its registered office; often it will be the address of a solicitor or property management company, or simply an accommodation address. But the key point is that any notice, or legal writ, is validly served if sent to that address, and the freeholder is not allowed to claim that it never came to his notice.

It is not necessary for the notice required by section 48 to be given in a separate document; it is enough if the name and address is clearly given as part of some other document such as a service charge demand. But if the necessary notice is not given, no payment of rent, service charge, or anything else is due to the freeholder; the leaseholder may lawfully withhold it until section 48 is complied with. But leaseholders withholding payments on this ground must be careful; once the notice is given, it has retrospective effect, so that all the money due to the freeholder then becomes due immediately. Any leaseholder withholding money on the grounds that section 48 has not been complied with should, therefore, make sure that he has the money easily available so that he can pay up if he has to.

c: Good management
The freeholder is under an obligation to ensure that his management responsibilities are carried out in a proper and appropriate way. Leaseholders can challenge the freeholder in court or at the LVT if they believe they can show that they are not receiving the standard of management to which they are entitled. This may be an expensive and lengthy process but it better than the alternative, sometimes resorted to by leaseholders, of withholding rent or service charge. This is risky because, whatever the shortcomings of the freeholder's management, it puts the leaseholders in breach of the conditions of their lease and, as such, demonstrably in the wrong (even if the freeholder may be in the wrong as well).

Withholding due payments is therefore not recommended unless the freeholder is so clearly at fault that arguably no payment is due - for instance, if the service being charged for has clearly not been provided at all (as opposed to being provided inadequately), or if there has been no 'section 48' notice (see above). If leaseholders choose to withhold payment, they are strongly advised to keep the money readily to hand so that they can pay up at once if the freeholder rectifies the problem; the danger otherwise is that they will be taken to court and required to pay immediately to avoid forfeiture (see below).

Powers of Leaseholders over Management

If leaseholders want a scrutiny of the standards of management of their flats, they have power under the Leasehold Reform, Housing and Urban Development Act 1993 to demand a management audit by an auditor acting on behalf of at least two-thirds of the qualifying leaseholders. Qualifying leaseholders are those with leases of residential property originally granted for 21 years or more and requiring them to contribute to the cost of services.

The purpose of the audit, the costs of which must be met by the leaseholders demanding it, is to discover whether the freeholder's duties are being carried out efficiently and effectively. The auditor is appointed by the leaseholders and must be either a qualified accountant or a qualified surveyor and must not live in the block concerned. The auditor has the right to demand papers from the freeholder and can go to court if they are not produced.

Leaseholders' Right to Manage

Leaseholders with long leases (those originally granted for 21 years or more) also have the right to take over management of their block if they wish. This applies to blocks of two or more flats (five or more if there is a resident landlord) and no substantial non-residential part. It does not apply if the freeholder is a local authority.

The leaseholders must first form a 'Right to Manage' company ('RtM' company), which is a limited company whose membership is confined to leaseholders and the freeholder. Before seeking to take over management the RtM company must advise all leaseholders of its intention and invite them to participate. Fourteen days after this invitation, and provided the RtM company includes at least half the eligible tenants (or both, if only two are eligible), it can serve a claim notice on the landlord (or on the Leasehold Valuation Tribunal, if the landlord is untraceable) giving at least four months' notice of its intention to take over the management. The landlord has a month to serve a counter-notice objecting to the claim, in which case the LVT will adjudicate. If no counter-notice is served, or if the LVT so decides, the RtM company duly takes over management.

The landlord must bring to an end as quickly as possible any existing management arrangements applying to the block. The RtM company takes over the landlord's management functions, including services, repairs, maintenance, improvements, and insurance. The landlord retains its role in respect of any flats without long leaseholders (for example, those let on assured tenancies), and continues to deal with forfeiture (for more on forfeiture see the section below 'If the lease is breached'). Essentially the RtM company steps into the landlord's shoes so far as management is concerned, and it is responsible to both the landlord and the individual leaseholders for the proper carrying out of its functions.

Many leases require the landlord's approval before certain things can be done, such as assigning the lease or sub-letting. The RtM company takes over this function from the landlord, but must consult the landlord before granting approval. If the landlord objects, the matter is referred to the LVT. It seems, however, that refusal of consent by the RtM is final and cannot be challenged by the landlord (although it might be challenged by the leaseholder in question on the ground that the relevant term of the lease is unenforceable). The RtM company has authority to enforce covenants in the lease, but not by means of forfeiture.

At first blush the power to take over management in this way may appear attractive. However, leaseholders should think very carefully before they commit themselves; there are some potential snags.

The biggest problem is one of enforcement. So long as all leaseholders are agreed about what needs to be done, and are all willing and able to meet their obligations (including that of paying for services), enforcement will not be an issue and all will be well. But if some individual leaseholders refuse to pay their share, or fail to abide by the covenants in their leases, the RtM company will have to act to enforce the leases and this may well be difficult. In the first place, any steps to enforce leases will pit neighbour against neighbour and are virtually certain to cause animosity in the block. Secondly, the powerful tool of forfeiture, or threatened forfeiture, is denied to a RtM company. Finally, the RtM company, unlike most freeholders, will not have any substantial financial resources that would allow it to pursue lengthy legal action against individual leaseholders.

There are other issues. The RtM company will depend on the voluntary efforts of its members, and experience shows that many people are not willing to put in the time and effort involved in attending meetings and carrying out essential administration. RtM companies have to operate under a special constitution laid down by the Government; the aim of this is to guarantee all leaseholders' rights to be involved, but because the constitution is a standard document applying to all cases it is likely that many leaseholders will find it clumsy and inflexible. Finally, there is the question of continuing relations with the freeholder, which will expect its interests as ultimate owner to be respected by the RtM company.

In short, leaseholders contemplating the formation of a RtM company need to be sure that they are committed not only for the immediate effort of setting it up but for the long haul of carrying out management in the future. They should also recognise that, no matter how united everyone may be to start with, sooner or later the issue of enforcement will rear its head. They should certainly get legal advice about their new responsibilities before committing themselves.

The law allows another remedy in extreme cases of mismanagement. A leaseholder can use the Landlord and Tenant Act 1987 to force the appointment of a managing agent to run the block instead of the freeholder. The leaseholder must serve a notice telling the freeholder what the problems are and warning that unless they are put right a Leasehold Valuation Tribunal will be asked to appoint a managing agent. The LVT may make such an order if it satisfied that it is 'just and convenient'; the Act mentions, as specific examples where this may apply, cases where the freeholder is in breach of obligations under the lease and cases where service charges are being levied in respect of work of a poor standard or an unnecessarily high standard. Note that the procedure is not available if the freeholder is a local authority, a registered housing association, or the Crown.

Recognised Tenants' Association

A recognised tenants' association (RTA), where there is one, has additional rights to be consulted about managing agents. The RTA can serve a notice requiring the freeholder to supply details of the managing agent and the terms of the management agreement. Recognised tenants' associations are more important, however, in connexion with service charges, so they are explained in the Chapter Three.

Leaseholders that are receiving a consistently poor or overpriced service may also wish to consider getting rid of the freeholder altogether by collective enfranchisement under the Leasehold Reform, Housing and Urban Development Act 1993.

Assignment of Leases

One of the most important characteristics of a lease - in marked contrast to most tenancies - is that it may be bought and sold. Usually, the freeholder has no say in this: the leaseholder may sell to whom he likes for the best price he can get, provided that the purchaser agrees to be bound by the terms of the lease. It is, however, usual for the lease to lay down that the freeholder must be informed of any change of leaseholder.

What actually happens when a lease is sold is that the vendor agrees to transfer to the buyer his rights and obligations under the lease. This is called 'assignment' of the lease. In some types of housing the freeholder has the right to intervene if an assignment is envisaged. The housing may, for instance, be reserved for a particular category of resident, such as the retired, so the freeholder is allowed to refuse consent to the assignment if the purchaser does not qualify.

It was mentioned above that the assignee takes over all the rights and responsibilities attaching to the lease. This means, for instance, that he takes responsibility for any arrears of service charge. This is why purchasers' solicitors go to such lengths to ensure that no arrears or other unusual obligations are outstanding.

If the Lease Is Breached

If the terms of a lease are broken, the party offended against can go to court. This may be the leaseholder, for instance if the freeholder has failed to carry out a repair. But it is normally the freeholder that takes the leaseholder to court, for failure to pay ground rent or service charges or for breach of some other requirement.

It is for the court, if satisfied that the lease has been breached, to decide what to do. The normal remedy will be that the offending party must pay compensation and that the breach (if it is still continuing) must be put right. It is also likely that the loser will be obliged to pay the winner's legal costs as well as his own, a penalty often considerably more severe that the requirement to pay compensation.

A much more severe remedy open to the freeholder if the leaseholder is in breach is forfeiture of the lease. This means what it says: the lease is forfeit to the freeholder. Forfeiture is sometimes threatened by the more aggressive class of freeholder but the good news for leaseholders is that in practice courts have shown themselves loath to grant it except in very serious cases. Since the Housing Act 1996 took effect, forfeiture for unpaid service charges has been made more difficult for freeholders; this is covered in the next Chapter.

Where forfeiture is threatened for any reason other than failure to pay rent (which, depending on the terms of the lease, may or may not include the service charge element), the freeholder must first serve a 'section 146 notice', so called after the relevant provision of the Law of Property Act 1925. In this he must state the nature of the breach of the lease, what action is required to put it right; if he wants monetary compensation for the breach, the notice must state this too.

Before the section 146 notice can be issued, it must be established that a breach of the lease has occurred. If the leaseholder has admitted the breach, the notice can be issued; otherwise, it must have been decided by a court, the LVT, or an independent arbitrator that the leaseholder is in breach. Moreover, the breach of the lease specified in the section 146 notice must have occurred during the twelve years preceding the notice. For breaches older than this, no valid section 146 notice can be served and so forfeiture is not available. If the notice is not complied with, the freeholder may proceed to forfeit; but the leaseholder may go to court for relief from forfeiture. In practice, courts have generally been willing to grant relief, but they cannot do so unless it is formally applied for. If the leaseholder, perhaps failing to realise the seriousness of the situation, fails to go to court and seek relief, the forfeiture will go ahead.

Forfeiture will be considered again in the next Chapter, which covers the special rules applying to forfeiture for failure to pay service charges.

The Government has announced that ultimately it intends to replace forfeiture by a different remedy that will recognise the value of the leaseholder's interest. Until this happens, however, forfeiture remains available and leaseholders must take care to avoid any possibility of its being used against them.

If the freeholder breaches the lease, the leaseholder can go to court and seek an order requiring the freeholder to remedy the breach, to pay damages, or to do both. The commonest type of breach complained of by leaseholders is failure to carry out repairs, and this explains why

113

action by leaseholders is less usual; they know that if they force the freeholder to do repairs the costs will be recovered through service charges. Legal action may be the best course if the dispute affects a single leaseholder; but if a number of leaseholders are involved they may well prefer to get rid of the freeholder altogether by collectively enfranchising their leases as described in Chapter Four.

Leasehold Valuation Tribunals
Several references have already been made to Leasehold Valuation Tribunals. These bodies operate throughout England and Wales. They are appointed jointly by the Lord Chancellor and (in England) the Environment Secretary and (in Wales) the Welsh Secretary. They perform a large number of quasi-judicial functions in relation to property, especially leasehold property, and feature frequently in this book.

19

OWNER OCCUPIERS AND SERVICE CHARGES

The Role of Service Charges

By far the commonest cause of dispute between leaseholders and freeholders is the provision of services and, especially, the levying of service charges. In extreme cases, leaseholders have been asked to contribute thousands of pounds towards the cost of major repairs, and have even suffered forfeiture of the lease if they are unable, or unwilling, to comply. Happily, such instances are rare; but even where the service charges are more moderate, they are often resented by leaseholders. The purpose of this Chapter is to explain the legitimate purpose of service charges and the legal obligations of both the leaseholder and the freeholder, and to offer some warnings about the circumstances where very high service charges are likely to be found.

The difference between long leases and tenancies (short-term and periodic) was set out earlier. One of its most important consequences is that services are paid for in a very different way. In a periodic or short-term tenancy, all the basic costs of providing and managing the housing are paid out of the rent. It is true that there will sometimes be a service charge as well, but it normally covers things such as the provision of heating or communal lighting - things that, however necessary they may be, are peripheral to the central function of providing housing. As a result, service charges in rented property are usually quite moderate and cause little argument.

Contrast the position in leasehold housing. In both types of housing, the landlord is under a legal obligation to the residents to keep the property in good condition and to carry out any work necessary for that purpose; but the landlord of rented property is expected to meet the costs from the rent, whereas the freeholder of leasehold stock has no rent to fall back on (apart from the normally negligible ground rent). How, then, are major costs to be met when they arise? The answer, of course, is from the service charge, which is, therefore, of central importance to the management of leasehold property.

115

From the freeholder's point of view, the logic of service charges is impeccable. It is perfectly reasonable for freeholders to point out:

- That leaseholders benefit from the work because it has maintained or improved their homes; and
- That the fact that the work has been done means that leaseholders will get a better price when they come to sell; and
- That people that own their homes freehold have to find the money to meet costs of this kind.

To sum up the freeholder's position: the costs have been incurred; the work is for the benefit of the leaseholders; so the leaseholders must pay.

Leaseholders can point out in reply that someone that owns his home freehold can make his own choice when and how to do the repair; he can put up with a slightly leaking roof if he cannot afford to repair it. But freeholders of leasehold property have no such discretion: they are obliged under the lease to do their repairs promptly and if they did not would be liable to legal action by any leaseholder.

So it is difficult for leaseholders to object to the principle of service charges or to ask the freeholder to refrain from carrying out work or to delay it. In short, the purchase of a lease means the acceptance of a commitment to pay the appropriate share of costs.

But does this mean that leaseholders have no scope to challenge or query service charges? No; under sections 18 to 30 of the Landlord and Tenant Act 1985, amended by the 1996 Housing Act and the 2002 Commonhold and Leasehold Reform Act they have extensive legal protection against improper or unreasonable charging by freeholders, and this is discussed later in the Chapter. First, however, we should look at how a typical service charge is made up.

The Components of a Service Charge

The lease will say how often service charges are levied: typically, six-monthly or annually. It is usual to collect the ground rent at the same time, but this is usually a fairly small component of the bill. The service charge proper will normally consist of three elements.

- **The management fee** is the charge made by the freeholder, or the freeholder's agent, to cover the administrative cost of providing the service and collecting the charge. Usually it will be much the same amount from one year to the next, but if major works have occurred the management fee will usually be higher to cover the extra costs of appointing and supervising contractors; 15% of the cost of the works is a common figure.

* **Direct costs (routine expenditure)** cover costs such as the supply of electricity to communal areas, building insurance, and the like. Again, these costs are likely to be fairly constant from year to year, so leaseholders know in advance roughly how much they are likely to have to pay.

* **Direct costs (exceptional expenditure)** cover costs that are likely to be irregular but heavy. They usually result from maintenance and repair, and it is because this component of the service charge is so unpredictable that it gives rise to so many problems. Where a house has been divided into leasehold flats, the freeholder's costs will usually be similar to what a normal home owner would be obliged to pay; in other words, the costs may well be in the thousands (for a new roof, say) but are unlikely to be higher. Even so, a charge of £5000 for a new roof, albeit divided between three or four flats, is still a major cost from the point of view of the individual leaseholder, especially if it is unexpected. The situation can be far worse in blocks of flats, where the costs of essential repair and maintenance may run into millions. Replacement of worn-out lifts, for example, is notoriously costly; and costs arising from structural defects are likely to be higher still. Suppose it costs £2 million to remove asbestos from a block of forty flats: the average cost per flat is £50 000, a figure that may well exceed the value of the individual flats, and is likely to be beyond the reach of most leaseholders. The problem of exceptionally high service charges is looked at in greater detail at the end of the chapter.

Unreasonable Service Charges
a: General Principles
Sections 18 to 30 of the Landlord and Tenant Act 1985, as amended by subsequent legislation, grant substantial protection to leaseholders of residential property. This protection was introduced after complaints of exploitation by unscrupulous leaseholders, who were alleged to be

carrying out unnecessary, or even fictitious, repairs at extravagant prices, whilst not providing the information that would have enabled leaseholders to query the bill. The general effect of the Act is to require freeholders to provide leaseholders with full information about service charges and to consult them before expensive works are carried out. It must be stressed, however, that although the Act protects leaseholders against sharp practice by freeholders, and will prevent the recovery of *unreasonable* costs, it will support freeholders, provided they have gone through the necessary formalities described below, in the recovery of their *reasonable* costs, even if those costs are high. To take the example used above of the removal of asbestos from a block of flats: the fact that the average cost per flat is as high as £50 000 does not, in itself, make the charge unreasonable - to make use of the Act, objecting leaseholders have to show, when they are notified that the work is to be carried out (not when the bills arrive), that it was not necessary or could have been carried out cheaper.

A few leases, namely those granted under the right to buy by local authorities or registered housing associations, have some additional protection under the Housing Act 1985 (see below), but sections 18 to 30 apply to all residential leases where the service charge depends on how much the freeholder spends. They set out the key rules that freeholders must observe in order to recover the cost, including overheads, of 'services, repairs or improvements, maintenance or insurance', as well as the freeholder's costs of management. Sections 18 to 30 only apply to service charges, not to other charges such as ground rent.

It should be noted that failure by leaseholders to pay the service charge does not relieve the freeholder of the obligation to provide the services. The freeholder's remedy is to sue the leaseholder for the outstanding charges, or even to seek forfeiture of the lease (see below).

Section 19 of the Act provides the key protection to leaseholders by laying down that service charges are recoverable only if they are 'reasonably incurred' and if the services or works are of a reasonable standard. This means that the charge:

-        must relate to some form of service, repair, maintenance, improvement, or insurance that the freeholder is required to provide under the lease;

- must be reasonable (that is, the landlord may not recover costs incurred unnecessarily or extravagantly);

- may cover overheads and management costs only if these too are reasonable.

In addition, the charge must normally be passed on to the leaseholders within 18 months of being incurred, and in some cases the freeholder must consult leaseholders before spending the money. These points are covered below.

The Housing Act 1996 gave leaseholders new powers to refer service charges to the Leasehold Valuation Tribunal (LVT). This is covered below (*Challenging Service Charges*).

b: Consultation with Leaseholders
Section 20 as amended by the 2002 Commonhold and Leasehold Reform Act provides extra protection where the cost of works is more than a certain limit. (£250 or more to the leaseholder). Costs above this level are irrecoverable unless the freeholder has taken steps to inform and consult tenants, although there are a exceptions in special cases (see below). If the leaseholders are not represented by a recognised tenants' association (for which see below) these steps are as follows:

Intention to carry out works: The landlord must write to all leaseholders stating the intention and reasons for carrying out work. There must be a notice period of 30 days.

Estimates At least two estimates must be obtained, of which at least one must be from someone wholly unconnected from the freeholder (obviously a building firm that the freeholder owns or works for is not 'wholly unconnected'; nor is the freeholder's managing agent. Arguably, even a building firm with which the freeholder has no formal connexion could be 'connected' with him if he gives it so much work that it depends on him and is thus subject to his influence)

Notification to leaseholders The freeholder must either display a copy of the estimates somewhere they are likely to be seen by everyone liable to pay the service charges or preferably send copies to everyone liable to pay the charge

Consultation The notification must describe the works to be carried out and must seek comments and observations, giving a deadline for replies and an address in the UK to which they may be sent. The deadline must be at least a month after the notice was sent or displayed.

Freeholder's response The freeholder must 'have regard' to representations received. This does not mean, of course, that the freeholder must do what the leaseholders say. It does mean, however, that the freeholder must consider any comments received, and good freeholders often demonstrate that they have done so by sending a reasoned reply (i.e. not a form letter or bare acknowledgment, but a letter that responds specifically to any points made), even though the Act does not require them to.

It was mentioned above that there are special cases in which these requirements can be set aside. If a service charge is challenged, it is defence for the freeholder to show that the works were so urgent that there was no time for proper consultation. It is also possible for freeholders to enter into long term agreements to carry out works or provide services over a period of years; if so, they must consult before the agreement is entered into but they need not consult separately before each particular element of expenditure under the agreement. Finally, the LVT has a general power to set aside the usual consultation requirements if it seems fair to do so.

Section 20 is important because it gives the leaseholders notification of any unusual items in the offing and gives them an opportunity to raise any concerns and objections. If the leaseholder has any reservations at all, it is vital that they be put before the freeholder at this stage. It is unlikely, in the event of legal action later, that courts or LVTs will support a leaseholder that raised no objection until the bill arrived.

It is surprisingly common for freeholders and their agents to fail to comply with the requirements of section 20. This comment applies not only where the freehold is owned by an individual or a relatively small organisation (where mistakes might be more understandable) but also where the freeholder is a large, well resourced body like a local authority (which should be well able to understand and carry out its legal duties).

As a result leaseholders are often paying service charges that are not due, so all leaseholders should, before paying a service charge containing unusual items, ensure that section 20, if it applies, has been scrupulously followed. If not, they can refuse to pay.

c: Other Protection for Leaseholders

Grant-aided works: If the freeholder has received a grant towards the cost of carrying out the works, the amount must be deducted from the service charge levied on leaseholders.

Late charging: Service charge bills may not normally include costs incurred more than eighteen months earlier. The freeholder may, however, notify leaseholders within the eighteen month period that they will have to pay a certain cost, and then bill them later. This may happen if, for instance, the freeholder is in dispute with a contractor about the level of a bill or the standard of work.

Pre-charging: Sometimes a lease will contain a provision allowing the freeholder to make a charge to cover future costs besides those already incurred. This practice, which is perfectly lawful in itself, may be in the interests of the leaseholders by spreading over a longer period the cost of major works. It is, however, subject to the same overall requirement of reasonableness.

Court costs: Section 20C provides protection against a specific abuse of the service charge system by freeholders. Previously, freeholders tended to regard their legal costs as part of the process of managing the housing and thus as recoverable from leaseholders. Such an attitude is not necessarily unreasonable: if, for instance, the freeholder is suing a builder for poor work, he is, in effect, acting on behalf of all the leaseholders and it is fair that they should pay any legal costs. But suppose the freeholder were involved in legal proceedings against one of the leaseholders: if the leaseholder lost, he would probably to be ordered to pay the freeholder's costs as well as his own; but if the freeholder lost, and had to pay both his own and the leaseholder's costs, he could simply, under the previous law, recover the money as part of the management element in the service charge. This meant that the freeholder was able to pursue legal action against leaseholders without fear of heavy legal costs in the event of defeat, the very factor that deters most people from too ready a resort to law. To prevent this, section 20C allows leaseholders to seek an order that the freeholder's legal costs must not be counted towards service charges.

Service charges held on trust: Section 42 of the Landlord and Tenant Act 1987 further strengthened the position of leaseholders by laying down that the freeholder, or the freeholder's agent, must hold service charge monies in a suitable interest-bearing trust fund that will ensure that the money is protected and cannot be seized by the freeholder's creditors if the freeholder goes bankrupt or into liquidation. However, public sector freeholders, notably local authorities and registered housing associations, are exempt from this requirement.

Administration charges: These are the freeholder's costs incurred in complying with leaseholders' requests for information and approvals under the terms of the lease. All such charges must be reasonable. Any demand for administration charges must be accompanied by a summary of leaseholders' rights and obligations in relation to them. The LVT has the power to decide whether or not an administration charge is payable, and if so, to whom and by whom together with the amount, date payable and the manner in which it is paid.

Ground rent: Strictly, this is not part of the service charge but as it is usually collected along with it, it is covered here. It will be specified in the lease and is usually a fairly modest annual sum in the order of £50 or £100. Leaseholders should note that, unlike the service charge and most other charges, the ground rent is not intended to compensate the freeholder for any costs or trouble; it is simply a payment by which the leaseholder recognises that ultimately the property belongs to the freeholder. Therefore freeholders are under no obligation to demonstrate that it is reasonable. But it is not payable unless the landlord has issued a formal request for it, which must specify the amount of the payment, the date on which the leaseholder is liable to pay it and the date (if different) on which it would have been payable under the lease. The date for payment must be at least 30 days and not more than 60 days after the date of the notice.

Insurance: Usually, any insurance required under the lease will be taken out by the freeholder and this is discussed below. Occasionally, however, the leaseholder will be required to take out insurance with a company nominated by the freeholder. If the leaseholder thinks he is getting a poor deal, he can apply to the county court or a Leasehold Valuation Tribunal which, if satisfied that the insurance is unsatisfactory or the premiums are unreasonably high, can order the freeholder to nominate another insurer.

'Period of Grace': When a dwelling is sold under the right to buy by a local authority or non-charitable housing association, the purchaser is given an estimate of service charges for the following five years. This estimate is the maximum recoverable during that time. Some purchasers under the right to buy have, however, had a very rude shock when the five year period of grace expires - see *Exceptionally High Service Charges* below.

d: The role of a recognised tenants' association

The tenants who are liable to pay for the provision of services may, if they wish, form a recognised tenants' association (RTA) under section 29 of the Landlord and Tenant Act 1985. Note that leaseholders count as tenants for this purpose (see Chapter One, where it explained that legally the two terms are interchangeable). If the freeholder refuses to give a notice recognising the RTA, it may apply for recognition to any member of the local Rent Assessment Committee panel ('Rent Assessment Committee' is the official term for a Leasehold Valuation Tribunal when it is carrying out certain functions, not otherwise relevant to leaseholders, under the Rent Act 1977).

An important benefit of having a RTA is that it has the right, at the beginning of the consultation process, to recommend persons or organisations that should be invited to submit estimates. However, the freeholder is under no obligation to accept these recommendations.

Another advantage is that the RTA can, whether the freeholder likes it or not, appoint a qualified surveyor to advise on matters relating to service charges. The surveyor has extensive rights to inspect the freeholder's documentation and take copies, and can enforce these rights in court if necessary.

Against these benefits must be set the principal disadvantage of having a RTA, namely that it weakens the freeholder's obligation to consult individual leaseholders. Where there is a RTA, the freeholder, instead of having to supply copies of the estimates to all leaseholders (or place copies where they are likely to be seen), merely has to send them to the secretary of the RTA, and the individual leaseholders must make do with summaries. Leaseholders - and for that matter, ordinary periodic tenants - should therefore weigh carefully the advantages and disadvantages of setting up a RTA. If they decide against, there is nothing to prevent them from forming an **unrecognised** tenants' (or leaseholders') association, which can represent their interests to the freeholder, provided that it is made clear that formal recognition under section 29 is not being sought.

Challenging Service Charges

The Landlord and Tenant Act not only allows leaseholders to take action against unreasonable behaviour by the freeholder; it also enables them to take the initiative. This is done in two ways: by giving leaseholders rights to demand information, and by allowing them to challenge the reasonableness of the charge.

Any demand for service charges must include details about leaseholders' rights and how they can challenge the charges. If this is not done the leaseholder may withhold payment without penalty.

a: Right to information
Freeholders must provide a written summary of costs counting towards the service charge. It must be sent to the leaseholder within six months of the end of the period it covers. The service charge need not be paid until the summary is provided.

The law lays down some minimum requirements for the summary. It must:
- cover all the costs incurred during the twelve months it covers, even if they were included in service charge bills of an earlier or later period (see above for late charging and pre-charging);
- show how the costs incurred by the freeholder are reflected in the service charges paid, or to be paid, by leaseholders;
- say whether it includes any work covered by a grant (see above);
- distinguish: (a) those costs incurred for which the freeholder was not billed during the period; (b) those for which he was billed and did not pay; (c) those for which he paid bills.

If it covers five or more dwellings, the summary must, in addition, be certified by a qualified accountant as being a fair summary, complying with the Act, and supported by appropriate documentation. The purpose of these rules is to put leaseholders in a position to challenge their service charges. After receiving the summary, the leaseholder has six months in which to ask the freeholder to make facilities available so that he can inspect the documents supporting the summary (bills, receipts, and so on) and take copies or extracts. The freeholder must make the facilities available within 21 days after such a request; the inspection itself must be free, although the freeholder can make a reasonable charge for the copies and extracts. Failure to provide these facilities, like failure to supply the summary, is punishable by a fine of up to £2500.

Very similar rules apply where the lease allows, or requires, the freeholder to take out insurance against certain contingencies, such as major repair, and to recover the premiums through the service charge. This is not unreasonable in itself and will, indeed, often be in the interests of leaseholders. The danger is, however, that the freeholder, knowing that the premiums are, in effect, being paid by someone else, has no incentive to shop around for the best deal. Section 30A of the Landlord and Tenant Act 1985 therefore lays down that leaseholders, or the secretary of the recognised tenants' association if there is one, may ask the freeholder for information about the policy. Failure to supply it, or to make facilities to inspect relevant documents available if requested to do so, is an offence incurring a fine of up to £2500.

It must be acknowledged that the rules allowing leaseholders to require information about service charges are, particularly in view of the £2500 fines, fairly onerous from the freeholder's point of view. It is the purpose of this book to inform leaseholders of their rights, not to make life difficult for freeholders: nevertheless, it must be admitted that if leaseholders wish to pursue a policy of confronting freeholders, and to cause them as much trouble as possible, sections 21, 22, and 30A offer plenty of scope.

b: Challenging a service charge

Any leaseholder liable to pay a service charge, and for that matter any freeholder levying one, may refer the charge to a Leasehold Valuation Tribunal to determine its reasonableness. This may be done at any time, even when the service in question is merely a proposal by the freeholder (for instance, for future major works). But the LVT will not consider a service charge if:

-       it has already been approved by a court; or

- if the leaseholder has agreed to refer it to arbitration; or
- if the leaseholder has agreed it.

The first of these exceptions is obvious and the second is unlikely to apply very often. The third one is the problem: leaseholders should be careful, in their dealings with freeholders, to say or do nothing that could be taken to imply that they agree with any service charge that is in any way doubtful.

The LVT will consider:

- whether a service charge is payable and if so when, how, and by whom;
- whether the freeholder's costs of services, repairs, maintenance, insurance, or management are reasonably incurred;
- whether the services or works are of a reasonable standard; and
- whether any payment required in advance is reasonable.

The fees for application to a LVT can be obtained from the LVT and will usually change annually. Appeal against a LVT decision is not to the courts but to the Lands Tribunal.

By section 19 of the Landlord and Tenant Act 1985, any service charge deemed unreasonable by the LVT is irrecoverable by the freeholder. The determination of service charges by the LVT also plays an important part in the rules governing the use of forfeiture to recover service charges. It is to this that we now turn.

Forfeiture for Unpaid Service Charges
Forfeiture was mentioned at the end of Chapter Two. Briefly, it is the right of the freeholder to resume possession of the property if the leaseholder breaches the lease.

By section 81 of the Housing Act 1996, forfeiture for an unpaid service charge is available to the freeholder only if:

- the leaseholder has agreed the charge; or
- the charge has been upheld through post-dispute arbitration or by the Leasehold Valuation Tribunal or a court.

Regarding the first of these, it is necessary only to reiterate the warning

126

to leaseholders to say or do nothing that could possibly be construed as representing their agreement to any service charge about whose legitimacy they have the slightest doubt.

Regarding the second, it should be noted that where the leaseholder has not agreed the service charge, proceedings before the LVT or a court or post-dispute arbitration are necessary before the freeholder can forfeit the lease.

A further requirement is that the amount of money involved must either exceed a certain amount or have been outstanding for a minimum period of time. The Government will set these limits by order. It is currently proposed that the minimum amount will be £350 and the minimum period three years, but this is yet to be confirmed. Note that it is necessary for only one of the requirements to be satisfied.

To sum up, before the leaseholder can forfeit:

- it must have been formally decided that the service charge is due,
- the amount must exceed the minimum amount or have been owed for the minimum time, and
- a section 146 notice must have been served (but this requirement does not apply if the service charge is reserved as rent).

The freeholder can still begin the process by issuing a section 146 notice (see Chapter Two) but it must state that the forfeiture cannot proceed until the requirements of section 81 have been met.

It remains to be seen how these new provisions will operate in practice. Their purpose is to prevent freeholders from using the draconian threat of forfeiture to pressurise leaseholders into paying disputed service charges, and to this extent the position of leaseholders has been greatly strengthened. The danger is that freeholders may respond by getting disputed charges before the LVT as quickly as possible so that forfeiture becomes available if the charges are upheld. Another concern is that some leaseholders, faced with service charges they are unwilling to pay but about which there is no dispute, may be unable to resist the temptation to invent spurious grounds for objection in order to deprive the freeholder of the weapon of forfeiture; this tactic is likely to provoke even relatively easy-going freeholders into legal action.

Once the leaseholder has agreed the service charge or it has been upheld by the LVT or a court or through arbitration, forfeiture becomes a serious threat and in this situation the advice can only be to pay the charge if at all possible. If, however, the leaseholder is unable to pay he may find it helpful to contact his mortgagee (if any). For the mortgagee, forfeiture is a disaster because it is likely to be left with a large unsecured debt on its hands, so many mortgagees in this situation will pay the service charges and add the cost to the outstanding mortgage. This does not solve the leaseholder's long term problem - that his lease commits him to payments he is unable to meet - but it will give him a little breathing space and may enable him to sell up and pay off his debts.

Some leaseholders, especially those of longer standing, may be living on fixed incomes and have very little cash to spare, even though their property is quite valuable. Sometimes their mortgage has been paid off altogether; even if it is still outstanding, it will probably be very small in relation to the value of the property. Leaseholders that find themselves in this 'property-rich, cash-poor' situation may find it helpful to look at equity release schemes, operated by a number of financial institutions.

Exceptionally High Service Charges

So far this Chapter has focused on service charges of normal proportions that, however unforeseen and unwelcome they may be, should be within the means of the great majority of leaseholders. A minority of leaseholders, however, face the much more serious problem of consistently very high service charges. Where the cause is sharp practice by the freeholder, or failure to observe the legal requirements, the leaseholder can look for protection to the Landlord and Tenant Act as described above. Often, however, the freeholder is not to blame: rather, the problem is that the work is genuinely necessary and unavoidably expensive. In this situation, and provided the landlord carefully follows the procedures laid down, the Landlord and Tenant Act offers no protection.

In what sort of housing is this most likely to occur? It is more likely to affect flats than houses because flats tend to contain potentially very expensive components such as lifts or communal arrangements for heating or ventilation. They are also more likely to have been built using construction methods or designs in vogue at one time but since found to lead to serious maintenance problems and high costs, whereas house building seems to be innately conservative and resistant to innovation: for instance, many blocks of flats contain asbestos, but very few houses.

All these problems apply to flats in general, but there is an additional

128

problem with blocks of flats owned by local authorities and housing associations: namely that, unlike blocks of flats developed by commercial owners for sale, they are likely to combine rented properties, let to periodic tenants in the usual way, with leasehold properties, sold at some point in the past under the right to buy or some similar scheme. These 'mixed managed' blocks present special problems for both categories of resident as well as the freeholder.

Clearly, there is no satisfactory way to resolve this problem. In a privately developed block, occupied wholly by leaseholders, the freeholder might possibly be prevailed upon to delay the repairs for a time if the leaseholders are prepared to put up with the poor conditions; but the Council can hardly be expected to take the same view when most of the residents are periodic tenants. Both the Council and the periodic tenants are likely to argue that the leaseholders are being asked to do no more than they agreed to do when they bought their leases.

In most cases, however, Councils will be able to say, quite truthfully, that they had no idea of the problem when the sale took place, in which case the court is likely to apply the established legal principle of *caveat emptor* - 'let the buyer beware'.

All this book can do is warn prospective leaseholders of the serious problems that can arise in a minority of cases, and suggest some of the questions that they should ask before signing the lease.

1 **What is the condition of the building as a whole?** No one would buy a house, or an individual flat, without looking closely at its condition and estimating how much money it may need to have spent on it. But, when a flat is being bought, whether it is purpose-built or a conversion, it is equally important to look at the entire building of which it forms a part. The vendor should be asked for copies of past service charges, the freeholder should be asked whether major work is likely in the foreseeable future and what it is likely to cost, and an independent surveyor should be asked to report.

2 **What is the leaseholder's liability?** The lease will specify what the leaseholder must pay for. Sometimes it will require him to contribute to things from which he does not benefit. For example, it is common for even ground floor leaseholders to be expected to contribute to the costs of the lifts; and some leaseholders, having

paid out of their own pockets to replace their windows, are outraged to discover, when the freeholder has the windows of the whole block renewed, that they are required to pay a share of the cost. Provisions such as these are much resented by many leaseholders, who argue that they are unfair; but the time to object to such unfairness is before signing the lease, not many years later when the bills come in. It is therefore essential that anyone proposing to enter into a lease should first consult a solicitor.

3   **Is there a 'period of grace' or other safeguard?** Right to buy leases contain an estimate of service charges for five years following the sale and that is the maximum that the Council may charge. Many purchasers, reassured by this, have signed the lease without paying much attention to the likely level of service charges thereafter, expecting perhaps to have sold at a profit and moved on before the five years expire. If so, they have been reminded of what many people forgot during the 1980s: that property prices can go down as well as up. In short, it is unwise to rely on a 'period of grace' to provide anything other than short-term relief; and in particular it is unwise to speculate on the future behaviour of the housing market.

4   **What are the prospects for resale?** Traditionally, the homeowner's last resort in the face of overwhelming financial problems is to sell up in the expectation that the proceeds will suffice to pay off the mortgage, settle other outstanding debts such as service charges, and still leave something over. The stagnant property market of the early 1990s upset many calculations of this kind, but the much stronger market of recent years means that mortgages are often appreciably less than the value of the property, so for many people selling up offers a way out. So it is important to assess the salability of the dwelling by asking whether future purchasers are likely to be put off by anything about the flat itself or the block and district to which it belongs, and above all whether mortgage lenders are likely to look on it favourably.

20

ENFRANCHISEMENT AND EXTENSION OF LEASES

It has always been, and still is, open to the freeholder and the leaseholder to negotiate lease extensions and variations. For instance, they might agree that the freeholder will buy the unexpired term of the lease from the leaseholder: but, because the freeholder and the leaseholder cannot be the same person, this will have the effect of extinguishing the lease and leave the freeholder in sole possession of the land as if the lease had never existed. Alternatively, the freeholder might agree to sell the freehold to the leaseholder: again, and for the same reason, this will extinguish the lease, but this time it is the former leaseholder that will be left in sole freehold possession. The sale of the freehold to the leaseholder is called 'enfranchisement' of the lease, because it is freed, or 'enfranchised', from the overriding freehold, and replaces it. A further possibility is that the freeholder and leaseholder may agree to extend the lease beyond its original term. If agreements of this kind are negotiated, it is entirely for the freeholder and leaseholder to settle the conditions and the price.

In recent years, however, the law has forced freeholders, in certain circumstances, to sell freeholds or extend leases, whether they wish to or not. This has been done by three pieces of legislation: the Leasehold Reform Act 1967, the Landlord and Tenant Act 1987, and the Leasehold Reform, Housing and Urban Development Act 1993 (although all three Acts have been amended by later legislation, particularly the Housing Act 1996 and the Commonhold and Leasehold Reform Act 2002). The Acts are dealt with in the order they were passed, which means that the most important right - that of leaseholders of flats - is left to last. This is fitting, because, as is explained below, it was a Parliamentary afterthought; the Government originally had no intention of granting such an important right.

But before looking at the legislation, it is important to establish why extension and enfranchisement are important to the average leaseholder.

Extension of a Lease Some enlightened freeholders automatically extend the lease whenever it is assigned, so that if a lease that was originally granted for 125 years is assigned after 30, the assignee gets a lease not for 95 years, as one might expect, but for 125. From the leaseholder's point of view, such an arrangement is extremely valuable because otherwise the lease represents a wasting asset, whose value will drop sharply as the end of the term approaches. The arrangement can also benefit the freeholder by making the lease more valuable at the time of its original sale. But most leases are unaffected by assignment and would expire on the originally determined date were it not for legislation that obliges freeholders, in certain circumstances, to grant a fresh 90 year lease to the leaseholder: this is described below.

Individual Enfranchisement of a Lease Legislation, described below, now allows the leaseholder to acquire the freehold, in certain circumstances, whether or not the freeholder agrees. If not for this, the leaseholder would find that his home had reverted to the ownership of the freeholder at the end the lease and he would have to buy it back (assuming the freeholder were willing to sell). The freeholder is, however, entitled to compensation.

Collective Enfranchisement of Leases The problem with leasehold enfranchisement is that the property concerned must be capable of being held on a freehold basis. Where it stands on a distinct and definable piece of land this does not present a problem: the freehold of the land is transferred to the leaseholder and, as explained in Chapter One, any buildings on it are automatically transferred too. But if the property is only part of a larger building, it may not be attached to its own unique piece of land in the same way, so individual enfranchisement is not available to flat owners. If they wish to enfranchise, therefore, they have to agree among themselves that a single person or body will buy the freehold on behalf of all of them, while they continue to hold leases of their individual flats. This is called 'collective enfranchisement', although this term is misleading because technically the leases have not been enfranchised at all: all that has happened is a change from the original freeholder to a new one nominated by the leaseholders.

Since the passage of the Commonhold and Leasehold Reform Act 2002, this new freeholder has to be a special type of organisation called a 'Right to Enfranchise' (or 'RtE') company.

Rights to Enfranchise and Extend Leases: General Principles

The remainder of this Chapter sets out what rights leaseholders have if they wish to extend or enfranchise their leases. It is stressed at the outset, however, that anyone contemplating such a step should obtain independent legal advice from a solicitor, and in most cases also from a valuer. This applies not only if the lease is being enfranchised or extended under one of the Acts, but also if it is being done voluntarily by agreement with the freeholder. The issues involved are potentially very complex and attempting to deal with them without expert advice could put your home at risk.

The Acts are available to what they describe as 'qualifying tenants': but the exact meaning of the term varies depending which right is being exercised under which Act. Usually, but not always, the term is defined in a way that excludes ordinary tenants and confines it to leaseholders. The key issue is the existence of a long lease (see below). Other former tests, relating to residence or the amount of rent, were abolished by the 2002 Act.

A Long Lease For most purposes under the Acts, the leaseholder must own a lease originally granted for at least 21 years. Note that this is the term when the lease was granted, not the period it still has to run, so that a 99 year lease granted in 1910 is still a long lease in 2009 even though it has only a few years to go. Recent legislation has put an end to a number of devices formerly inserted into leases by freeholders in order to avoid having to extend or enfranchise leases.

Some were bizarre: leases were made terminable on extraneous events, such as royal marriages or death's, because the lease was not regarded as long if it depended on an event that could occur at any time. These evasions have been of no effect since the 1993 Act, which provides that leases containing them shall be treated as long leases.

Exemptions There are various exemptions from the Acts.

-       If the freeholder is a charitable housing trust and the dwelling is provided as part of its charitable work, the leaseholder can neither extend nor enfranchise the lease (unless the charity agrees).
-       The Acts do not apply to business leases. This applies even if a dwelling is included: for instance, if the lease of a shop includes the flat above it.
-       The Acts do not apply if the property is within the precincts of a

cathedral or owned by the Crown (however, it is possible that the Crown authorities will agree to a voluntary extension or enfranchisement of the lease). Some properties owned by the National Trust are also exempt.

- Other exemptions apply not across the board but to particular types of transaction. These are covered as the various Acts are discussed below.

Leasehold Reform Act 1967: Leases of Houses

The first legislation to deal with leasehold extension and enfranchisement was the Leasehold Reform Act 1967. This Act is still in force, but is not relevant to most residential leaseholders, who will get more benefit from later legislation. It can therefore be dealt with fairly briefly.

The Act relates only to residential leases of houses - not flats. With certain exceptions, a leaseholder qualifies to use it if he has held for at least two years a lease originally granted for 21 years or more. The Act allows qualifying leaseholders to acquire the freehold of their homes, or, if they prefer, extend the lease for 50 years.

The usual exemptions (see above) apply to the 1967 Act. In addition, it does not apply to most shared ownership leases granted by housing associations.

Most leaseholders qualifying to make use of the 1967 Act have long since done so, because the benefits of owning the freehold outweigh the drawback of having to pay the freeholder the difference (usually not very great) between the freehold and leasehold value of the house.

Generally speaking, therefore, remaining leasehold houses will be those to which the Act does not apply, either because the freeholder is exempt or because the house is attached to other property. The last point is an important limitation on the 1967 Act: if the land on which the house stands is shared by any other property not covered by the lease, however small it may be compared with the house, the Act cannot be used. It may, however, be possible for the leaseholder of such a house to use the new rights in the Leasehold Reform, Housing and Urban Development Act 1993.

The procedure for enfranchisement under the 1967 Act is as follows.

- The leaseholder serves a notice on the freeholder stating that he wishes to claim the freehold (or extend the lease). This notice should give particulars of the property and the lease.

- Within two months, the freeholder must send a counter notice that either accepts the leaseholder's claim or gives reasons for rejecting it. The freeholder may ask the leaseholder for a deposit of £25 or thrice the annual ground rent, whichever is more, and for proof that he holds the lease and meets the residence test. The leaseholder has 14 days to produce the money and 21 days to produce the proof.

- If the freeholder does not submit a counter notice within two months, the leaseholder's claim is automatically accepted. If the freeholder's counter notice unfairly rejects the leaseholder's claim, the leaseholder may apply to the county court.

Obviously, the freeholder is justified in rejecting the claim if the property does not come under the Act or if the leaseholder does not qualify. In addition, the freeholder may reject the claim if he acquired the house before 18th February 1966 and needs the house, on expiry of the lease, as a home for himself or a member of his family. He may also refuse to extend the lease (but not to enfranchise it) if he plans to redevelop the property.

Once it has been established that the leaseholder may enfranchise, a price must be agreed; if this is not possible, it will be set by a leasehold valuation tribunal. The Act lays down that the price should be the value of the freehold if it were being sold willingly but on the assumption that the lease were continuing and would be renewable under the Act. In effect, this formula means that the leaseholder is obliged to pay for what he is acquiring (the freehold) but not for what he has already got (the lease). Once a price has been agreed, or set by tribunal, either the freeholder or the leaseholder has one month to serve a notice on the other requiring him to complete. The freeholder must convey the freehold as a fee simple absolute, or (as a non-lawyer would say) outright.

Landlord and Tenant Act 1987: First Refusal and Mismanagement

The Landlord and Tenant Act 1987 was chiefly concerned with enabling leaseholders to protect themselves against unreasonable service charges, and it made numerous amendments to tighten the rules originally laid down in the Landlord and Tenant Act 1985 (see Chapter Three).

In addition, it granted leaseholders the important right of first refusal if the freehold of their property is sold. It also allowed leaseholders to acquire the freehold if the property is being mismanaged: however, this right is little used because of the difficult procedures involved, and although it remains on the statute book it is likely to fall into complete disuse because the 1993 Act has now given leaseholders the same right without having to prove mismanagement.

a: First refusal

The right of first refusal was granted in order to stop the practice of selling freeholds, without any reference to the leaseholders or other occupiers, from one person or organisation to another so that leaseholders were often completely in the dark about who the ultimate freeholder was (when this sort of thing went on the eventual freeholder often turned out to be a company existing on paper only and based somewhere completely inaccessible like the Cayman Islands. The right of first refusal remains important because it is sometimes available when ordinary collective enfranchisement, under the 1993 Act, is not possible.

The 1987 Act says that if the freeholder intends to sell the freehold he must first offer it to the leaseholders and other qualifying tenants. There are, however, some exceptions: the Act does not apply if the freeholder is selling to a member of his family, or if he lives in the block himself; nor does it apply if the block is not chiefly residential. In addition, virtually all public sector freeholders are excluded from the Act: this means local authorities, registered housing associations, and various other bodies. It is, however, unlikely that this sort of body will wish to sell its freehold. But if none of these exceptions applies, and if the majority of qualifying tenants (including leaseholders) wish to buy, they must be given the opportunity to meet the freeholder's price. For the purpose of defining a 'majority' there can be only one qualifying tenant in respect of each flat: in other words, joint tenants (or joint leaseholders) have only one 'vote' between them, and must agree between themselves how it will be used.

'Qualifying tenants' are:

- tenants entitled to a Fair Rent under the 1977 Rent Act: that is, most tenants of self-contained dwellings holding a tenancy originally

136

granted on or before 14th January 1989, but excluding council tenants; and

- leaseholders, except for business leaseholders (the normal 21 year minimum does not apply).

If the qualifying tenants and freeholder cannot agree terms for the sale, the freeholder is able to sell to someone else. However, the qualifying tenants must be informed of this sale and, most importantly, of the price. They then have the right to buy the freehold from the new owner at whatever price he paid. This is designed to stop the original freeholder from asking the qualifying tenants for an excessive price that they are bound to reject, then selling to someone else at a lower price. Similarly, if the freeholder carries out a sale without informing the qualifying tenants, they have the right to buy from the new freeholder for the same price that he paid. Procedure under the 1987 for the right of first refusal is as follows.

* The freeholder notifies all qualifying tenants of his desire to sell and of the price at which he is willing to do so (including any non-monetary element). The notice must state the proposed method of sale: for instance, by conveyance or by auction.

* The freeholder must give the qualifying tenants at least two months to respond; and, if they say they wish to buy, at least a further two months (28 days if the sale is to be by auction) to come up with a nominee purchaser to acquire the freehold on their behalf. This could conceivably be in an individual or an organisation that already exists, but is much likelier to be a company set up especially for the purpose by the qualifying tenants, and under their control.

* During this period, the landlord and the qualifying tenants may wish to take the opportunity to negotiate the price.

* If a majority of the qualifying tenants have put forward a nominee purchaser and agreed with the freeholder on a price, the freeholder may not sell to anyone else.

* If the qualifying tenants fail to put forward a nominee purchaser,

or if a mutually acceptable price is not agreed, the freeholder has twelve months to sell to someone else in accordance with the original notice (by auction, if that was the method specified; and in any other case for a price not less than that originally offered to the qualifying tenants). If no sale has taken place within twelve months, the freeholder must start the procedure again from scratch if he wishes to sell.

b: Mismanagement: the right to enfranchise

As mentioned above, the 1987 Act is designed mainly to protect leaseholders against mismanagement and sharp practice by freeholders. It therefore gives them the power of collective enfranchisement against a freeholder guilty of serious or repeated breach of his obligations. The power is available to long leaseholders, but a leaseholder does not qualify to use this part of the Act if he owns long leases of three or more flats in the block.

Moreover, this part of the 1987 Act does not apply where the freeholder is the Crown or a public body such as a local authority or a registered housing association. Nor does it apply when the freeholder resides in the property himself. It is available only where two-thirds or more of the flats in the block are let on long leases, and in blocks of ten flats or fewer a higher proportion is required. The court can make an order transferring the freehold to the leaseholders' nominee only if a manager appointed (see Chapter Two) by a court or LVT has controlled the premises for at least two years, unless the leaseholders can show both

- that the freeholder is and is likely to remain in breach of his obligations under the lease; and
- that the mere appointment of a manager would be an inadequate remedy.

All these restrictions suggest that the Act envisages that enfranchisement on grounds of mismanagement is very much a last resort; indeed, it is necessary for the leaseholders to take their case to court and get permission before they can proceed. The right was seldom used and, although it remains available in theory, in practice it has been superseded by the 1993 Act, which gives most leaseholders the right of collective enfranchisement whatever the standard of management and with no need for a court order. Nevertheless, it is just possible there is a body of leaseholders somewhere willing to use the 1987 Act rather than the 1993 Act. The procedures for collective enfranchisement following mismanagement are therefore briefly set out here, with a warning that the general recommendation to employ a solicitor applies with special emphasis if this route is chosen.

- At least two-thirds of the qualifying leaseholders must serve a preliminary notice informing the freeholder that they intend to go to court to acquire the freehold. The notice must give the names and addresses of the leaseholder and the grounds for their application; the freeholder should also be given a reasonable deadline to rectify the problems if it is possible for him to do so.

- The leaseholders must apply to the court, giving their reasons for dissatisfaction and requesting an order to transfer the freehold to their nominee purchaser (probably, as with other forms of collective enfranchisement, a company set up for the purpose).

- If satisfied that it is fair to do so, the court will transfer the block to the nominee purchaser. The price will have to be agreed by the leaseholders and the freeholder; or, if (as is likely) this is not possible, by a Leasehold Valuation Tribunal. The price will be the value of the freehold on the assumption that all the leases are to continue: there will be no additional 'marriage value' (see below), and this is one of the few reasons for preferring to use the 1987 Act rather than the 1993 Act.

Leasehold Reform, Housing and Urban Development Act 1993: Collective Enfranchisement and Lease Extension

The 1993 Act greatly extended the rights of leaseholders: its passage through Parliament was, indeed, strongly contested by large private freeholders, who claimed that it was unfair to them as property owners. It made a number of adjustments, dealt with above, to existing rights under the 1967 and 1987 Acts; in addition, it created two new rights for leaseholders of flats. These are the right to collective enfranchisement, and the right to extend individual leases.

a: Collective enfranchisement under the 1993 Act

In outline, the right to collective enfranchisement under the 1993 Act is similar to, but much easier than, collective enfranchisement under the 1987 Act. Under both schemes, qualifying leaseholders choose a purchaser to whom the freeholder can be forced to sell; but under the 1993 Act there is no need for a court order and no need to show that there has been mismanagement.

The 1993 Act is available to long leaseholders, provided that at least two-thirds of the flats are let on long leases and at least half the eligible leaseholders are involved.

However, the block may not be enfranchised if it falls within the normal exemptions, or if it is not chiefly residential, or if it is a house converted into four flats or fewer with a resident freeholder who owned the freehold before the conversion. Even if there is a resident freeholder, however, the scheme applies to houses converted into five flats or more and to purpose-built blocks even if they contain only two flats.

There are special provisions for any parts of the building that are occupied by people or organisations other than qualifying leaseholders. Some flats may be let to periodic tenants, for instance, and a block that faces a main road may well contain shop units on the ground floor. Any such parts may, and in some cases must, be leased back to the original freeholder when the block is acquired. 'Leaseback', as it is called, is mandatory for any flats let to periodic tenants (secure or assured) by a local authority or a registered housing association. This means that they can continue as council (or association) tenants, and do not lose any legal rights. It is up to the freeholder (not the leaseholders) whether he wants a leaseback of other flats or premises, such as business units or flats occupied by non-qualifying leaseholders. Unless the parties agree otherwise, leaseback is for 999 years at a notional rent - in other words, on terms typical of residential leases, and discussed in Chapters One and Two.

The leaseholders must choose a purchaser. Formerly, this could be any individual or organisation that had the confidence of the others and was willing to undertake the role. The 2002 Act has, however, tightened the rules by providing that only a 'Right to Enfranchise' ('RtE') company can take over the freehold. This protects leaseholders' rights by ensuring that the enfranchisee is a body in which they all have a right to be involved, but the Government has taken powers to lay down what the constitution of the RtE company must be, and it is likely that many leaseholders will find the prescribed constitution unwieldy and inflexible.

Setting up and running the RtE company is only one of the responsibilities in which collective enfranchisement will involve leaseholders. They will also have to pay both their own and the freeholder's legal and professional costs. And above all, they must pay the purchase price of the freehold, which, unless they come to an agreement with the freeholder, will be decided by a leasehold valuation tribunal in accordance with rules laid down in the Act. These say that the price consists of two components: the open market value and the 'marriage value'.

According to the formula in the Act, the **open market value** should reflect the income the freeholder would have received from rents plus the prospect of regaining possession of the parts of the building currently let. How much this is will depend on how the building is being used now. If, as will often be the case, it consists wholly of flats let on long leases with many years to run, the open market value will probably be low because ground rents are usually very modest and the prospect of regaining possession is a distant one and of correspondingly little value. But if the building contains lucrative business or periodic tenancies, perhaps quite short term, and if the freeholder elects not to have these leased back, the open market value will be substantial.

The other component in the price, the **'marriage value'**, is based on the assumption that, combined (as they will be after enfranchisement), the leases and the freehold have a greater value than they would if sold separately. The Act says the freeholder is entitled to half this amount. In most cases, however, especially where the leases have a long time to run, the marriage value will be low, and where a lease has more than 80 years to run the marriage value will be disregarded. Altogether the costs of enfranchisement may be considerable. It is therefore prudent for leaseholders to explore the ground before committing themselves. This can be done by any qualifying leaseholder by serving a notice on the freeholder (or whomever the leaseholder pays rent to) under section 11 of the Act. Such a notice obliges the freeholder to disclose, within 28 days, information that will be relevant to any sale, such as title deeds, surveyor's reports, planning restrictions, and so on. This will allow the leaseholders to take an informed view of whether they wish to go for collective enfranchisement and, if so, on what terms. At this stage, they should take their time and think it over carefully, for if they proceed further they will be obliged to pay the freeholder's legal costs if they later decide to withdraw. It may be appropriate, too, at this stage, for the leaseholders to ask the freeholder whether he is prepared to consider a voluntary sale without forcing all concerned to go through the somewhat elaborate procedures laid down by the 1993 Act. A reasonable freeholder, since he will be aware that he can be forced to sell anyway, may well be willing to discuss this.

If the leaseholders decide to go ahead with collective enfranchisement under the 1993 Act, they must form a 'Right to Enfranchise' ('RtE') company. The purpose of the company is to act as the vehicle for the enfranchisement and subsequently to own the freehold of the block.

Every RtE company has to operate in accordance with a constitution (the 'memorandum and articles') laid down by Government. The aim is to ensure that all leaseholders have a fair chance to take part, but it is likely that many leaseholders will find that the constitution laid down for them is extremely bureaucratic and unwieldy, especially when it is remembered that many enfranchisements will be carried out in small blocks where they may be only a dozen leaseholders or even fewer.

All qualifying leaseholders are entitled to be members of the RtE company, but in practice it is controlled by 'participating members', namely those leaseholders that have served on the company a 'participation notice'. When the company is set up all qualifying leaseholders must be sent a formal notice inviting them to participate by serving such a notice. Once the enfranchisement takes place, membership of the RtE company is confined to participating members.

The RtE company serves an initial notice (also called a 'section 13 notice') giving the names and addresses of the leaseholders involved and exactly specifying what property they wish to enfranchise and which parts, if any, they will lease back. The notice must also propose a price, and give the freeholder at least two months to reply. Once the initial notice has been served, the freeholder may not sell the freehold to any third party.

From now on, the RtE company handles proceedings on behalf of the leaseholders. The freeholder may require the RtE company to provide evidence to show that the participating leaseholders are qualified under the Act. If the RtE company does not respond within 21 days, the freeholder may in some circumstances treat the initial notice as being withdrawn.

By the date specified in the initial notice, the freeholder must serve a counter notice either accepting the leaseholders' right to enfranchise or giving reasons for rejecting it. The freeholder must also state whether he accepts the details of the leaseholders' proposal as regards price and exactly what is to be included in the sale, and must say whether he wishes to lease back any parts of the property (in addition to those where leaseback is mandatory). The freeholder may refuse to exercise his right to lease back parts of the premises let on lucrative business lets because the effect of this will be to increase the price and, perhaps, deter the leaseholders from continuing. In the unlikely event that most of the leaseholders' leases have less than five years to run, the freeholder has the right to stop the enfranchisement if he can satisfy a court that he intends to redevelop the block.

The intention of the Act is that after the freeholder's counter notice the parties will attempt to resolve any differences, so that the sale of the freehold can proceed on agreed terms. Often, however, agreement will be impossible and in that case the matters in dispute are referred to a leasehold valuation tribunal. Such a referral must take place at least two months, and not more than six months, after the freeholder's counter notice; if no agreement is reached, and no referral made, after six months, the initial notice will be deemed withdrawn.

Once the terms have been settled, the parties have two months to exchange contracts. At the end of this time, the nominee purchaser has a further two months to ask a court to transfer the freehold on the terms agreed (or determined by the tribunal); or the freeholder may ask the court to rule that the initial notice shall be treated as being withdrawn.

To sum up, the procedure is complex and demanding, which is why it has been little used even though several years have passed since it became available under the 1993 Act. The 2002 Act has made the process more favourable to leaseholders in some ways, but these improvements are more than offset by the further layer of difficulty added by the new requirement to set up a RtE company. All in all, it seems likely that these procedures will not be much used, but their existence may be helpful in persuading freeholders to negotiate seriously if leaseholders want to buy the freehold.

b: Lease extension under the 1993 Act

Although the right to collective enfranchisement, as created by the 1993 Act, is of great importance because it makes a fundamental shift in the relationship between freeholders and leaseholders, the complex procedures mean that it is likely to be relatively seldom used. On the other hand, the right to a new lease, which was also created (for flat owners) by the 1993 Act, is likely to prove of immense practical benefit to thousands of leaseholders, not least because it can be exercised on an individual basis. It is ironic that this, the most valuable right leaseholders derive from the 1993 Act, was something of a Parliamentary afterthought. The original intention was to create the right to collective enfranchisement, with individual lease extensions as very much a second best option available only to leaseholders that for some reason were disqualified from collective enfranchisement. But as the legislation made its way through Parliament the right to extend leases was granted to more and more categories of leaseholder, and by the time the Act became law it had become a general right.

The principle is similar to the right to lease extension that house owners enjoy under the 1967 Act. Anyone that has owned for at least two years a long lease of a flat qualifies to extend it under the 1993 Act. The former low rent test and residence test were abolished by the 2002 Act. The freeholder is required to grant a new lease running for the remainder of the term of the old lease plus an additional 90 years, so that if the old lease had 40 years to go the new one will be granted for 130. In other respects, however, the terms of the new lease will be the same as, or very similar to, the old one.

The leaseholder will have to pay the freeholder a sum consisting of two components calculated in accordance with rules set out in the Act. The first represents the reduction in the market value of the freehold that results because the freeholder will now have to wait to regain possession for 90 years longer than would otherwise have been the case. The less time the old lease had to run, the higher this component is likely to be. The second component is the 'marriage value', reflecting the higher value of a longer lease. As with collective enfranchisement, the freeholder is entitled to 50% of the marriage value, but it is disregarded altogether if the old lease has more than 80 years to go.

A leaseholder who is contemplating a lease extension should begin by serving a preliminary notice on the freeholder. This has the same function as with collective enfranchisement: it commits the leaseholder to nothing, but requires the freeholder to supply within 28 days the information that will enable the leaseholder to decide whether to go ahead.

The procedure is modelled on that for collective enfranchisement:

- The leaseholder serves an initial notice (a 'section 42 notice') on the freeholder. This must give details of the property concerned as well as of the leaseholder and his claim to qualify to use the 1993 Act. It must state how much the leaseholder proposes to pay, and set a date, at least two months ahead, by which the freeholder must reply. Once the notice has been served, the leaseholder must allow the freeholder to have access to the flat for the purpose of valuation.

- The freeholder must either agree that the leaseholder qualifies under the Act, or give reasons for disagreeing. If the freeholder agrees that the leaseholder is qualified to extend the lease, he may still suggest a that price of the new lease, or its other terms, should be different to the leaseholder's proposals. The freeholder can go to court for permission to reject the extension entirely if the current lease has less than five years to run and the freeholder then intends to redevelop the property.

- The freeholder and leaseholder should then attempt to resolve any differences by negotiation. If agreement is not reached, the question may be referred to the leasehold valuation tribunal at lease two months, and not less than six months, after the freeholder's counter notice. If, six months after the counter notice, there is neither an agreement nor a referral to a tribunal, the leaseholder's initial notice will be deemed withdrawn. In this event the leaseholder is liable for any reasonable expenses incurred by the freeholder.

- Once the terms are settled, either by negotiation or by the tribunal, the parties have two months to exchange contracts. If exchange does not take place during this period, the leaseholder has a further two months to apply to court for an order extending the lease on the terms agreed (or laid down by a tribunal).

It should be noted that collective enfranchisement takes priority over individual lease extensions, so that the effect of an initial notice of collective enfranchisement is to freeze, for the time being, any current claims to extend leases. If the collective enfranchisement fails to go ahead, the extension claims resume where they left off.

21

RELATIONSHIP BREAKDOWN AND HOUSING RIGHTS

When a relationship breaks down, whether the people in question are married or not, problems can often occur in relation to the property that was home. The rights of people will depend mainly on whether they are married or not, whether there are children involved and the legal status of individuals in the home.

Housing rights in an emergency

In the main, it is women who suffer from domestic violence. This section refers to women but the rights are the same for men.

If you are women and have been threatened by a man and are forced to leave your home then there are several possibilities for action in an emergency. The first of these is either going to a women's refuge. These provide shelter, advice and emotional support for women and children. These refuges will always try to admit you and as a result are sometimes crowded. They will always try to find you somewhere to live in the longer term. Refuges have a 24-hour telephone service if you need to find somewhere. For addresses see *useful addresses* at the back of this book.

Approaching the council

A person suffering domestic violence who has been forced to flee can approach the local council and ask for help as a homeless person. Councils will demand proof of violence and you will need to get evidence from a professional person, such as doctor or social worker or police. The council decides whether or not it has a duty to help you and you should seek advice if they refuse. Some councils, but not all will offer help to battered women. If you are accepted as homeless then the council should not send you back to the area where the violence began.

Obtaining a court order

Another course of action in an emergency is to obtain a court order against the man you live with. Courts can issue orders stating that a man:

- Should not assault you or harass you
- Not to assault any children living with you
- To leave the home and not to return
- To keep a certain distance from your home or any other place where your children go regularly.
- To let you back in your home if you have been excluded.

If you believe a court order would help you should get advice on where to find a solicitor or law centre that deals with these types of applications to the court. Certain orders are harder to get than others, such as exclusion orders. Matters need to be very serious indeed before such an order will be made. However, you will be advised of this when approaching a solicitor or law centre.

Failure to obey the terms and conditions laid down in the order can lead to arrest for contempt and a fine or even imprisonment.

Long term rights to the home

Long term rights to stay in a home depend on a number of circumstances. If you are married and the ownership or tenancy of the property is in joint names you have equal rights to live in the property. If it is owned then you will have a right to a share of the proceeds if it is sold. In certain circumstances have a right to more (or less) than a half share, or to the tenancy in your name after divorce.

If you are married but the ownership or tenancy is in one name only there are laws to protect the rights of the other party. Courts have the power to decide who has the ownership or rights over the matrimonial home, even if the property is held in one persons name only. This can also apply to people who were married but are now divorced and to those who were planning to get married within three years of their engagement.

Spouses who are not the owner or tenant of the home have a right to stay there. The court has the power to exclude either of the spouses, even if they are sole or joint owner or tenant. If your husband has left and stopped paying the rent or mortgage payments, the landlord or building society is obliged to accept payments from you, if you wish to make them, even if the property is not in your name. If the home is owned by your husband then you can register your right to live in it. This prevents your husband selling the home before the court has decided who should live there. And also prevents him taking out a second mortgage on the property without your knowledge. This is known as 'registering a charge' on the home. The court also has the power to transfer a fully protected private tenancy, an assured tenancy or a council or housing association tenancy from one partner to another.

If the matrimonial home is owner occupied and proceedings have started for a divorce, the court will decide how the value of the property will be divided up. The law recognises that, even if the property is in the husbands name only, the wife has a right to a share in its value, that she often makes a large unpaid contribution through housework or looking after children and that this should be recognised in divorce proceedings. The court looks at a number of things when reaching a decision:

- The income and resources of both partners
- The needs of you and your husband
- The standard of living that you and your husband had before the marital breakdown
- Ages of partners and length of marriage
- Contributions to the welfare of the family
- Conduct of partners
- Loss of benefits that you might have had if the marriage had not have broken down.

The court also has to consider whether there is any way that they can make a 'clean break' between you and you husband so that there are no further financial ties between you.

In certain circumstances, the court can order sale of the matrimonial home and the distribution of proceed between partners.

If you are not married
If you are not married then your rights will depend on who is the tenant or the owner of the home.

Tenants
If a tenancy is in joint names then you both have equal rights to the home. You can exclude your partner temporarily as we have seen by a

court order. If you are a council tenant then you may want to see if you can get the council to rehouse you. You should get advice on this from an independent agency (see useful addresses).

If the tenancy is in your partners name only then the other person can apply for the right to stay there, for their partner to be excluded or for the tenancy to be transferred.

Home owners

If you live in an owner occupied property you and you partner may have certain rights to a share of the property even if you are not married.

If the home is jointly owned then you have a clear right to a share in its value. If one person has contributed moiré than the other then a court can decide that an equal share is unfair. The court cannot order the transfer of the ownership of property but it can order the sale and distribution of the proceeds.

If the home is in one persons name there is no automatic right to live in the home, even if there are children. However, a solicitor acting on your behalf can argue that by virtue of marriage and contribution you should be allowed to stay there and be entitled to a share.

22

HOUSING ADVICE

General advice
Citizens Advice Bureaus, which are situated throughout the U.K., provide advice on all problems, including housing and other matters such as legal, welfare benefits and relationship breakdown. If appropriate they can refer you for more specialist help to a solicitor or advice agency. This advice is free of charge. To find a local office, look in the telephone directory under National Association of Citizens Advice Bureau.

Housing Advice Centres
In many areas there are specialist advice centres offering housing aid and advice. The service they offer varies from one-off information to detailed help over a long period. There are two main types of housing advice centres, Local council housing aid centres which can advise on all kinds of problems, although they will not be able to take action against their own council. Independent housing aid centres may be better equipped to do this. These centres can offer detailed assistance over a length of time and also one-off advice. There are a number of independent housing aid centres throughout the country operated by Shelter. You should contact Shelter for you're nearest centre.

Other specialist advice
Law centres-they offer free advice and can sometimes represent you in court. They can usually advise on all aspects of law and also advise battered women. They cannot, however, take divorce cases. For this you will need a solicitor. Shelter can provide a list of law centres.

For advice on welfare rights you should try the local council, who may employ a welfare rights advisor. Advisers can also contact the advice line which is run by the Child Poverty Action Group. For women's rights the Women's Aid Federation England and Welsh Women's Aid refer battered women, with or without children, to refuges. They can put you in touch with sympathetic solicitors and local women's aid groups and can offer a range of other advice, such as welfare benefits.

For immigration advice, the Joint Council for the Welfare of Immigrants offers advice on all types of problems connected with immigration and nationality. The United Kingdom Immigrants Advisory Service offers advice and help on problems with immigration. The Refugee Council has an advice service for refugees and asylum seekers.

Advice from solicitors

Solicitors can advise you on all aspects of the law, represent you in certain courts and, if necessary, get a barrister to represent you. It is best to find a solicitor who specialises in housing rights as they usually have a wider knowledge of specific areas. You can get a list of solicitors who specialise in housing law from the Community Legal Service (CLS) Directory in your local library. The list is also on the CLS website. Citizens Advice Bureaus can also supply specialist solicitor details.

Free advice and help

The legal Help Scheme can pay for up to two hours worth of free advice and assistance and for matrimonial cases up to three hours. The scheme is means tested and you must come withy the limits of the scheme to qualify. For details of the scheme you should approach a Citizens Advice Bureau or a solicitors practice operating the scheme. You must have reasonable grounds for defending an action. In certain cases, if you succeed in obtaining cash compensation then you may have to pay a proportion of it back, this is known as the *statutory charge*.

Appendix 1 – Useful addresses

Age Concern England
Freepost SWB 30375
Ashburton
Devon
TQ13 7ZZ
0800 00 99 66

Building Societies Association
6th Floor, York House
23 Kingsway
London
WC2B 6UJ
0207 520 5900

Child Poverty Action Group
94 White Lion Street
London N1 9PF
020 7837 7979

Equality and Human Rights Commission
3 More London
Riverside Tooley Street
London
SE1 2RG
020 3117 0235

Consumers Association
2 Marylebone Road
London NW1 4DF
020 7770 7000

Disability Alliance
Universal House
88-94 Wentworth Street
London E1 7SA
020 7247 8776

Equal Opportunities Commission
Arndale House
Arndale Centre
Manchester
M4 3EQ
0845 601 5901

Federation of Black Housing Organisations
Second Floor
1 King Edwards Road
London E9 7SF
020 8533 7053

Gay and Lesbian Switchboard
020 7837 7324

Homeless Link
Gateway House
Milverton Street
London SE11 4AP
020 7840 4430

Immigration Advisory Service
County House
190 Great Dover Street
London SE1 4YB
0844 794 4000

The Independent Housing Ombudsman
81 Aldwych
London WC2B 4HN
0300 111 3000

Leasehold Advisory Service
31 Worship Street
London EC2A 2DX
0207 374 5380

Legal Action Group
242 Pentonville Road
London N1 9UN
020 7403 3888

National Council for Civil Liberties (Liberty)
21 Tabard Street
London SE1 4LA
020 7403 3888

Prisoners Wives and Families Association (PACT)
Park Place
12 Lawn Lane
Vauxhall
London
SW8 1UD
020 7735 9535

Women's Aid Federation Helpline
PO Box 391
Bristol BS9 7WS
0117 944 4411

Emerald Publishing
www.emeraldpublishing.co.uk

106 Ladysmith Road
Brighton BN2 4EG

Other titles in the Emerald Series:

Law
Guide to Bankruptcy
Conducting Your Own Court case
Guide to Consumer law
Creating a Will
Guide to Family Law
Guide to Employment Law
Guide to European Union Law
Guide to Health and Safety Law
Guide to Criminal Law
Guide to Landlord and Tenant Law
Guide to the English Legal System
Guide to Housing Law
Guide to Marriage and Divorce
Guide to The Civil Partnerships Act
Guide to The Law of Contract
The Path to Justice
You and Your Legal Rights

Health
Guide to Combating Child Obesity
Asthma Begins at Home

Music
How to Survive and Succeed in the Music Industry

General
A Practical Guide to Obtaining Probate
A Practical Guide to Residential Conveyancing
Writing The Perfect CV
Keeping Books and Accounts-A Small Business Guide
Business Start Up-A Guide for New Business
Finding Asperger Syndrome in the Family-A Book of Answers

For details of the above titles published by Emerald go to:

www.emeraldpublishing.co.uk